THE ADDISON-WESLEY NETWORKING BASICS SERIES

Designing Storage Area Networks

The Addison-Wesley Networking Basics Series

The Addison-Wesley Networking Basics Series is a set of concise, hands-on guides to today's key technologies and protocols in computer networking. Each book in the series covers a focused topic and explains the steps required to implement and work with specific technologies and tools in network programming, administration, and security. Providing practical, problem-solving information, these books are written by practicing professionals who have mastered complex network challenges.

Thomas Clark, *Designing Storage Area Networks: A Practical Reference for Implementing Fibre Channel SANs,* 0-201-61584-3

Geoff Mulligan, *Removing the SPAM: Email Processing and Filtering,* 0-201-37957-0

Richard Shea, *L2TP: Implementation and Operation,* 0-201-60448-5

John W. Stewart III, *BGP4: Inter-Domain Routing in the Internet,* 0-201-37951-1

Brian Tung, *Kerberos: A Network Authentication System,* 0-201-37924-4

Andrew F. Ward, *Connecting to the Internet: A Practical Guide about LAN-Internet Connectivity,* 0-201-37956-2

Visit the Series Web site for new title information:
http://www.awl.com/cseng/networkingbasics/

THE ADDISON-WESLEY NETWORKING BASICS SERIES

Designing Storage Area Networks

A Practical Reference for Implementing Fibre Channel SANs

Tom Clark

Addison-Wesley
An Imprint of Addison Wesley Longman, Inc.
Reading, Massachusetts • Harlow, England • Menlo Park, California
Berkeley, California • Don Mills, Ontario • Sydney • Bonn
Amsterdam • Tokyo • Mexico City

Many of the designations used by manufacturers and sellers to distinguish their products are claimed as trademarks. Where those designations appear in this book, and Addison Wesley Longman, Inc. was aware of a trademark claim, the designations have been printed in initial capital letters or in all capitals.

The author and publisher have taken care in the preparation of this book, but make no expressed or implied warranty of any kind and assume no responsibility for errors or omissions. No liability is assumed for incidental or consequential damages in connection with or arising out of the use of the information or programs contained herein.

The publisher offers discounts on this book when ordered in quantity for special sales. For more information, please contact:

AWL Direct Sales
Addison Wesley Longman, Inc.
One Jacob Way
Reading, Massachusetts 01867
(781) 944-3700

Visit A–W on the Web: www.awl.com/cseng/

Library of Congress Cataloging-in-Publication Data

Clark, Tom, 1947
    Designing storage area networks : a practical reference for
implementing Fibre Channel SANs / Tom Clark.
        p.   cm. — (The Addison-Wesley networking basics series)
    Includes bibliographical references.
        1. Computer networks.   2. Information storage and retrieval
systems.   3. Internetworking (Telecommunication)   I. Title.
    II. Series.
    TK5105.5.C547   1999
    004.6—dc21   99–33181
                                                            CIP

ISBN 0-201-61584-3
Text printed on recycled paper
1 2 3 4 5 6 7 8 9 10—CRW—02010099
First printing, August 1999

Contents

Preface

This book is a practical guide for designing and implementing storage area networks, or SANs. Storage networking based on Fibre Channel technology is a relatively new phenomenon, and although there is ample material for study in the form of standards documents and standards interpretations, few practical references are available. This book attempts to achieve a balance between the technical detail required to understand the basic principles of Fibre Channel SANs and the most useful features the technology currently offers for concretely solving storage problems in enterprise data networks. This relatively short text is, therefore, not an exhaustive treatment either of Fibre Channel specifications or for the reader. Ideally, the reader will gain both a working knowledge of the building blocks of a SAN and a framework for understanding how storage issues can be addressed with real products. For a more in-depth treatment of standards, the listing in the bibliography and Robert Kembel's *Fibre Channel Consultant* series are strongly recommended.

The sheer volume of data generated by today's commercial and academic institutions has created a storage crisis for information technology (IT) managers and administrators. Although larger-capacity disk drives absorb part of the growing data load, connecting the requisite number of disks to file and application servers by traditional means has become increasingly difficult. Providing the bandwidth to keep up with the users' requests for data is also a continual challenge, as are allocating sufficient time and bandwidth for backing up data to tape. These issues are stressing the capabilities of storage infrastructures that have been in place for the past 20 years and are giving rise to new solutions outside the boundaries of traditional server/storage connectivity.

This book is intended for IT managers, administrators, consultants, and technical staff responsible for data storage and considering Fibre Channel SANs as a means to resolve bandwidth, capacity, and management issues. Storage area networking represents a major shift from previous storage models, since it introduces new networking products and concepts between servers and storage. The text does not assume prior knowledge of networking concepts and discusses the most essential aspects of networking as they apply to SANs. In addition to storage and server administrators, networking professionals who use SANs as an extension of the local and wide area enterprise network may also find value in this book. For these readers, discussions of basic server and storage concepts should assist in bridging the gap between networking and storage worlds.

Fibre Channel is a standards-based architecture that provides gigabit speeds, long distances, and support for millions of devices in an extended network. Fibre Channel has become synonymous with storage area networking, due to its support of the protocols most optimized for moving data to and from disk and its inherent networking capabilities. Although SAN "fossils" can be found in older mainframe and minicomputer environments, the concept of storage networking (and the acronym SAN itself) did not enter mainstream consciousness until Fibre Channel products appeared in the market.

Organization of This Book

This book highlights the attributes of Fibre Channel technology as embodied by useful products and explores the various topologies that are available to build SANs for specific application needs. The first two chapters establish a foundation for understanding the profound change that networking brings to the traditional storage paradigm. Chapters 3 and 4 have more technical content for readers desiring a glimpse into the inner workings of the Fibre Channel architecture. Capabilities of various SAN building blocks are discussed in Chapter 5 so that the reader can place them into a coherent and effective design. Since in the real world, no installation is flawless, Chapter 6 describes basic problem-isolation techniques, as well as methods that facilitate day-to-day operations. Chapter 7 gives an overview of SAN management, including network and volume management. Chapter 8 presents examples of Fibre Channel SAN configurations for video, prepress, tape backup, and other applications and explains the selection of SAN components based on bandwidth, distance, and redundancy requirements. The text concludes with a brief discussion of future trends in Fibre Channel SAN technology.

Although the discussions of Fibre Channel products and storage management applications in this text are vendor-neutral (Web sites of vendors for specific product lines are listed in Appendix B), the reader will not mistake the general tone of Fibre Channel advocacy throughout the work. It is difficult to be completely impartial about a technology that resolves so many real and pressing problems, especially when few viable alternatives exist. Fibre Channel SANs will not satisfy every data storage requirement but will, with proper design and implementation, address the majority of them.

Acknowledgments

Condensing an entire networking architecture and product development into a concise practical guide has presented considerable challenges. Accomplishing this within a few months' time was, as it turns out, an unrealistic but finally attainable goal. When deciding to write a book, as with having a child, no one tells you in advance that your life will change profoundly for the duration. Fortunately, I've had some excellent help. For pointing out omissions, suggesting improvements and clarifications, and agonizing through my sometimes blatant disregard for elementary principles of grammar, syntax, and punctuation, I have several people to thank.

My thanks, first of all, to Mary Hart of Addison Wesley Longman. She initially approached me with this project and managed it to completion. Her professionalism in organizing the reviewers, follow-through on outstanding issues, and constant support facilitated finishing the manuscript for publication.

I would also like to thank the people whom Mary Hart rallied to review the book proposal and various drafts. From general technical observations and suggestions to detailed corrections of language usage, the reviewers were quite helpful in getting the work into a final manuscript. My thanks to Lawrence Krantz of EMC Corporation, Paul Massiglia of Quantum Corporation, Dennis Miller of BEST Consulting, Mart Molle of the University of California at Riverside, Stephen Rago of CrosStor, and Brad Stamas of StorageTek.

My immediate and grossly underpaid editor is my wife, Lou, who patiently read through multiple revisions of each chapter and now knows more about Fibre Channel SANs than she ever anticipated. Her always useful suggestions helped ensure the book's readability, even through the more technical sections.

I would like to thank all of my Vixel Corporation coworkers who have, by their example, encouraged me to greater efforts in an exciting and very demanding new technology. My special thanks also to Karen Collis, Mike James, Donna Jollay, and Mike Thompson for reviewing the manuscript and providing their insights and support.

Finally, for helping me appreciate and keep foremost the standpoint of the ultimate consumers of data communications technology—the end users—I would like to acknowledge the very positive influence of my former coworkers, Herb Gulley, Dale Hawkinson, Steve Lamonte, and Tom Staggs.

Tom Clark
Seattle
tclark@vixel.com

1

Introduction

1.1 A Paradigm Shift

Storage area networks, or SANs, represent a major shift from the traditional server-to-disk data model. In the vast majority of enterprise and information networks, file servers are at the center of data access. The data itself exists in various forms—as e-mail, word-processing documents, spreadsheets, engineering diagrams, digital video, and so on—and typically resides on magnetic or optical disks. Driven by end-user requests, servers are perpetually reading and writing data files on disk and wrapping the data in the appropriate network protocol for transport to the user.

The traditional model of data access requires each request for data to pass through the file server that, in effect, owns all of the data on its attached disks. On the network side, the server is the focal point for network-generated requests for data; on the storage side, the server is the focal point for all disk activity required to service those requests.

Built on the Small Computer Systems Interface (SCSI) parallel bus architecture, this legacy model links servers to storage arrays with fixed, dedicated connections. Data on a particular disk can normally be accessed via the SCSI bus only by a single server. The amount of data available to that server, in turn, is limited by the number of disks supported by the bus and the number of buses supported by the server.

If the server or any of its SCSI connections to disks fails, access to data is lost. For mission-critical networks, this potential for catastrophic loss is unacceptable. Access to data is, for the enterprise, as obligatory as dial tone. Loss of access is, very directly, loss of business.

1

The fact that this server-centric model does not lend itself to the high-availability and high-volume requirements of enterprise networks is the primary impetus for changing the server/storage relationship.

Storage area networks are in the forefront of this change. SANs introduce the flexibility of networking to servers and storage and, by eliminating the dedicated connection between server and disk, enable a data-centric universe to expand. The speed, capacity, and network flexibility of SANs are based primarily on Fibre Channel architecture. Fibre Channel provides scalable bandwidth—currently at 100MBps per second—redundant data paths, long distances (to 10 km), and high device population.

Like any emerging infrastructure, storage area networking has had a long incubation period during which the technology has existed only in the form of proposals, standards drafts, and a few early market products. Fibre Channel, for example, was initially formulated in the late 1980s and has existed as a proposed ANSI (American National Standards Institute) standard since 1995. The first Fibre Channel products appeared in volume in 1996. Now, dozens of companies are manufacturing adapter cards, transceivers, hubs, and switches specifically for the SAN market. As of the spring of 1999, all major vendors of file servers, disk storage, and tape were shipping SAN-enabled products. By 2002, the SAN market is expected to exceed $2 billion.

Many corporate and information networks have unknowingly implemented SAN solutions, simply by selecting a particular vendor's server and storage products. Sun Microsystems, for example, shipped thousands of SPARC (Scalable Processor Architecture) configurations based on quarter-speed, or 266Mbps, Fibre Channel connections. Later, Sun's Photon server/storage products incorporated full-speed Fibre Channel—1.0625 Gbps—and Arbitrated Loop. Sun Microsystems, however, was not selling SANs. Sun had been marketing servers and storage that, to enhance storage access and throughput, necessarily incorporated SAN components. Consequently, a large installed base of storage area networks has existed for several years, even before SANs entered popular consciousness in the industry trade press.

Until the advent of SANs, the connection between server and storage had escaped the general onslaught that networking has waged against the rest of data communications. Routers, switches, routing protocols, any-to-any connectivity, mesh topologies, and so on, are alien concepts in the traditional server/storage paradigm. As long as the user networks requesting data were slower than the servers' ability to retrieve and store data to disk, there was no pressing need to reengineer the server-to-storage link.

Real problems occur, however, when user networks become populous and fast and place increasing demands on server resources. Competitive performance for server technology is now cast in tens of thousands of I/O (input/output) transactions, volumes of data in terabytes, and requirements for server/storage data rates at hundreds of megabytes per second. Backing up massive amounts of data to tape or other media within a reasonable time frame has become increasingly difficult. Multimedia applications are placing new demands on storage and bandwidth. The accelerating market acceptance of SAN concepts and products reveals that these problems are pervasive in enterprise networks and that Fibre Channel SANs are providing workable solutions.

Solving complex storage issues with SAN technology is no trivial task. Designing storage networks requires careful analysis of the storage application and the ability of SAN components to perform as required. Features and capabilities that exist as Fibre Channel standards may not yet exist as real products. The standards themselves may define some abstract capabilities that have little immediate relationship to real-world implementations. And unfortunately, depending on the marketing philosophy of particular vendors, some manufacturers of SAN products may exaggerate the capabilities of their products to gain a superficial market advantage.

For the IT (information technology) professional investigating SAN technology to solve practical problems, the first step in designing and implementing SANs is to understand what is real and what is not. Fibre Channel, for example, is often described as a 200MBps full-duplex transport. In reality, no full-duplex applications can drive 100MB concurrently in both directions. For practical network design purposes, each gigabit Fibre Channel pipe can, depending on the vendor's implementation, provide up to 100MBps sustained throughput. Once this expectation is set, it is then a matter of selecting the appropriate SAN topologies, based on actual bandwidth requirements.

1.2 Text Overview

This book focuses on the practical implementation of SANs and, when necessary, indicates when abstract features diverge from practical benefits. The value of any new technology is not realized until real products solve real problems. SANs have already been deployed to solve tape backup, data mining, disaster recovery, server clustering, and other applications that exceed the capability of traditional server/storage connectivity. Leveraging the practical experience that has already been won will facilitate designing and implementing viable solutions for these and other applications.

Chapter 2, Storage and Networking Concepts, provides an overview of basic networking concepts and positions the relationship of SANs to both traditional bus architecture and a complementary storage solution: network-attached storage (NAS). Since IT professionals responsible for server and storage management may not be familiar with internetworking concepts, attention is given to those principles of networking that are common to SAN architecture. Readers who are already familiar with basic networking may want to fast-forward through Section 2.1.

Chapter 3, Fibre Channel Internals, explores the main gigabit features and protocols that enable SANs. Fibre Channel is a layered network architecture, providing rules for the physical movement of data at high speeds and the interface between this high-speed transport and the upper-level application protocols that it services. Although some discussion of Fibre Channel standards is required to understand the underlying principles, other useful texts and the Fibre Channel standards themselves are available for the reader seeking more detailed explanations. Due to its technical content, this chapter will be of less interest to readers seeking an overview of SANs without delving into byte-level descriptions.

Chapter 4, SAN Topologies, discusses the three Fibre Channel topologies that are most commonly used for SAN implementations: point-to-point, Arbitrated Loop, and fabrics. Because Arbitrated Loop configurations represent the largest installed base of storage networks, its unique protocol requirements are examined in more detail. Fabric switches offer enhanced features that, in combination with loops, offer powerful design options for SANs.

Chapter 5, Fibre Channel Products, describes the major hardware and software components of a SAN. Adapters, controllers, switches, and hubs all play distinct roles in building the physical interconnect and in maintaining the proper transport protocol for server/storage conversations. True to the competitive nature of the market, functionality of SAN products may vary from vendor to vendor. In addition, the vendors themselves are changing, via acquisitions, strategic alliances, or fatalities due to competition. Consequently, the discussion of specific SAN products is limited, where possible, to the features that are most useful for implementing SANs, regardless of what features particular vendors have advertised.

Chapter 6, Problem Isolation in SANs, gives a brief overview of the unique diagnostic challenges SANs offer. The diagnostic tool of choice for SAN environments is the Fibre Channel analyzer. Analyzers, however, are expensive and require considerable expertise to operate and interpret. This chapter also provides simple problem-isolation techniques that are useful for diagnosing link-level problems and protocol-related events.

Management of SANs is critical for maintaining high availability of storage and server resources. Chapter 7, Management of SANs, reviews the various management strategies that have been proposed for the SAN interconnect, as well as more global management of files, disk volumes, and backup. Traditional management of servers and disk arrays is limited largely to fan, temperature, and power supply status. The introduction of networking behind the server brings an added complexity and so has required more sophisticated management techniques. At a higher level, integration of SAN device management with file and volume management is leading to umbrella applications that promise total control over the SAN.

Chapter 8, Application Studies, examines seven practical applications for SAN technology: full-motion video, prepress operations, LAN-free and server-free tape backup, server clustering, Internet service providers, campus storage networks, and disaster recovery. Each of these applications presents specific problems for storage networking and by example offers insight into the parameters that should be observed for proper SAN implementation. The design criteria of any network should be application-driven. Determining how much data is required, from what sources, and at what speed is often more difficult than finding the appropriate building blocks to fulfill those needs. As the application studies demonstrate, SANs provide a flexible architecture for satisfying a wide variety of requirements, including bandwidth, distance, population, and redundancy.

Chapter 9, Fibre Channel Futures, discusses new capabilities that are under development. Fibre Channel is an evolving gigabit technology. Proposals are already being presented for 2Gb and 4Gb speeds, as well as autosensing techniques for mixed-speed environments. Fibre Channel–to–ATM interconnect is another area of interest, since it enables high-speed universal data access between storage networks across wide area networks. As these and other initiatives materialize as useful products, the SAN designer will have a much wider array of options available for satisfying the enterprise's growing appetite for data.

1.3 Summary

- The predominant server-to-storage connection is parallel SCSI cabling. A parallel cabling scheme is limiting, since typically only a single server has access to its attached storage. The parallel SCSI model is server-centric.

- Storage area networks represent a paradigm shift from legacy SCSI configurations. SANs provide scalable bandwidth and the flexibility of networking that enable a data-centric model to emerge.

- SANs may be built with other architectures but are based primarily on Fibre Channel. Fibre Channel SANs are already deployed in enterprise networks and have proven functionality.

- Separating Fibre Channel features that exist only as standards from those engineered into available products is an essential first step for designing and implementing SANs.

2

Storage and Networking Concepts

Computer networks allow multiple users to share resources and to access common data. The largest computer network, the Internet, provides access for millions of users over a global infrastructure. E-mail, file transfer, Web browsing, and other applications are enabled by a complex, any-to-any topology that ultimately terminates at the sources of common data: file and application servers. The servers, in turn, store and retrieve user data and programs to and from disk arrays. E-mail, for example, is routed by the internetwork to the destination mail server, which stores messages on disk until the recipient retrieves them. Figure 2-1 illustrates a typical data communications network. In this example, each file server has externally attached disk arrays.

A server's ability to service thousands of requests for data quickly is governed by several factors: the processing speed of the server, the speed of its connection to the network, and the bandwidth available for moving data to and from disk. As both processor speed and network bandwidth have increased, additional pressure is placed on the connection between server and disk. In response, new technologies have evolved to enhance both disk performance and server-to-storage throughput.

In addition to raw bandwidth requirements, other factors are forcing change in the traditional server/storage model. File and application servers have become critical components of information and business networks. High availability of data requires redundancy of both disk and server resources. Storage requirements are growing at an unprecedented rate, thanks largely to the fusion of text and graphical

7

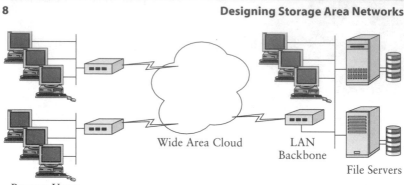

Figure 2-1 *A simple data communications network*

applications. And the growing volume of data from multiple servers must be backed up to tape or optical storage for archiving and disaster recovery. These new requirements are not easily satisfied by legacy server/storage implementations.

The conventional method for connecting storage to a server is defined by the **SCSI (Small Computer Systems Interface)** bus architecture. A SCSI (pronounced "scuzzy") bus is a dedicated, parallel cabling scheme between a server and one or more disk arrays, as shown in Figure 2-2. The SCSI bus architecture is not a networking topology; it was not designed to link multiple hosts on a common data path. Although it is physically possible to link two servers to 15 disk arrays with SCSI parallel cabling, the resulting conglomeration of cables and terminators presents a considerable configuration, maintenance, and diagnostic challenge.

Two alternatives to traditional SCSI bus configuration have been offered by **network-attached storage (NAS)** and **storage area networks (SANs)**. The common denominator of both solutions is the introduction of networking concepts to the server/storage paradigm. Networking resolves a number of problems inherent in the SCSI bus model and presents a few new ones of its own.

To help you better understand the unique features that networking offers to servers and storage, the following discussion reviews network topologies that have developed in the wide area network (WAN) and local area network (LAN) in front of the server. Understanding basic networking concepts is essential for understanding the possibilities and

File Server   External Storage via SCSI Bus

Figure 2-2 *SCSI bus configuration*

issues presented by SANs. Limitations of the SCSI bus are then examined, followed by an overview of NAS and SAN strategies.

2.1 Networking in Front of the Server

Over the past 30 years, a variety of data network structures has evolved to link computer resources. Networks may be defined by protocol—for example, SNA and IP—and geography—for example, local, metropolitan, and wide area. Regardless of the specific means used to move data from one user to another, network infrastructures generally follow a hierarchy that extends from the physical layer up through the end-user application.

The abstract reference for this hierarchy is the seven-layer **OSI (Open System Interconnection) Reference Model** (Table 2-1). Although individual network protocols may deviate from the OSI Reference Model, it is a useful structure for understanding the basic features of networking. As it is passed down by an application for transmission across the network, user data is wrapped in successive envelopes of information, roughly corresponding to the layers represented in the table.

A file transfer, for example, would acquire an information envelope on the file's format (layer 6), information useful for maintaining the file transfer session between sender and recipient (layer 5), information for acknowledgments that blocks of the file had been received (layer 4), network addressing information (layer 3), information about the type of media on which the data was originated (layer 2), and, finally, encoding to place the data on the physical transport (layer 1). At the receiving end, each envelope would be verified and removed by the

Table 2-1 OSI Reference Model

Layer	Number and Name	Function
7	Application	E-mail, file transfer interface
6	Presentation	Data formatting: application-specific
5	Session	End-to-end session control: NetBIOS (Network Basic Input/Output System), application-specific
4	Transport	Transmission control: TCP, UDP, SPX
3	Network	Routing protocol: IP, IPX
2	Data Link	Access method: Ethernet, Token Ring, FDDI
1	Physical	Transport: twisted pair, fiber optics, coax

target until the data comprising the original file could be passed to the upper layers for reconstruction.

Network protocols, such as TCP/IP (Transmission Control Protocol/Internet Protocol) and Novell IPX/SPX, enable data transfer for both local area and wide area networks. In more complex data networks, data wrapped in network protocols may pass through multiple LAN and WAN segments before arriving at the final destination.

Local area networks are typically built to link computers at a single site, such as an office building or a data center. LANs provide connectivity over a variety of physical links, including twisted-pair wiring, fiber optics, coaxial cable, and wireless transmitters. These media correspond to layer 1 of the OSI Reference Model.

The most prevalent LAN transport is Ethernet over twisted-pair copper wiring (see Figure 2-3). Ethernet transmission rates are 10 Mbps (megabits per second), 100Mbps (also known as Fast Ethernet), and 1,000Mbps (Gigabit Ethernet). 10Mbps and 100Mbps speeds are most common, with effective data rates of slightly more than 1MBps (megabytes per second) and 12MBps, respectively. These data rates decline as more computers are attached to the same Ethernet segment. Ethernet is so ubiquitous that modern office complexes are prewired with both phone and Ethernet jacks in every office and cubicle.

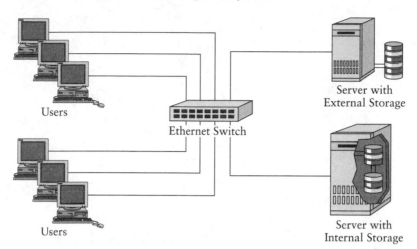

Figure 2-3 *A LAN segment using switched Ethernet*

In addition to the physical connection between computers, Ethernet provides a unique access method so that multiple users can share the same media. Ethernet uses collision detection to sense whether several computers on the same cable are sending data at the same time. If a collision occurs, each computer stops transmitting and tries again after a timing interval. Although this scheme has a certain brute force character, Ethernet is economical to deploy and has captured the LAN market from Token Ring and other competing topologies.

Due to transmission characteristics of twisted-pair wiring and Ethernet's access method, LANs are normally limited to a single building. To share computer resources with remote sites, wide area networks use telecommunications lines, microwave, or satellite to transmit data.

Routers are an essential ingredient of both LANs and WANs. As shown in Figure 2-4, routers sit on the local LAN segment and move data from one local segment to another and to the telecommunications carrier, such as AT&T or WorldCom, for remote sites. This connection to the carrier is often depicted as a cloud, since any number of microwaves, satellites, or land lines could be used to move data from the local site to the remote. On the other side of the cloud, a phone line connects to a remote router, which in turn services the remote computer users. As with Ethernet, WAN topologies provide access methods to ensure the orderly transmission of data from one site to another.

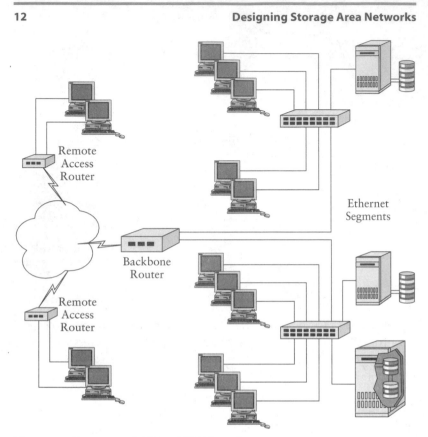

Figure 2-4 *Routers in LAN and WAN configurations*

Point-to-Point Protocol (PPP), Frame Relay, and asynchronous transfer mode (ATM) specify different data communications methods for
the WAN.

Several fundamental principles of networking are common to both
LAN and WAN technologies. Networking principles include

- Serial transport
- Access method
- Addressing
- Packetizing of data
- Routing of packets
- Upper-layer protocol support

Since these networking fundamentals also form the foundation of storage area networks, it is important to understand how each contributes to the network infrastructure and enables the paradigm shift now occurring in server-to-storage connectivity.

2.1.1 Serial Transport

Networking is a serial transport. The digital ones and zeros that comprise all data are transmitted sequentially, one bit at a time, from source to destination. Serial transmission enables data to be shipped over longer distances with fewer resources at a faster data rate. Serial transmission over fiber-optic cabling, for example, can extend tens of kilometers; over satellite, hundreds of kilometers. Alternatively, a parallel transport, such as a parallel printer interface, must use multiple lines to send groups of bits concurrently. Due to electrical and clocking considerations, parallel transmission is severely limited in distance, usually to less than 25 meters.

2.1.2 Access Method

A networked device requires an access method to gain control of the transport media. Ethernet uses carrier sense and collision detection, whereas Token Ring provides a token that can be claimed by only one user at a time. Regardless of the underlying transport, a form of media access control is essential for ensuring data integrity.

2.1.3 Addressing

Each device on a network must have a unique identity, which is established by a unique address. Depending on the upper-layer protocols that a device supports, a single networked computer may also have a unique address corresponding to each protocol layer.

An Ethernet interface card in a PC, for example, has a unique MAC (media access control) address that is assigned by the manufacturer. The 6-byte MAC address is used when data is exchanged between computers on the same LAN segment. If a user wishes to communicate with another device on a different segment, a network protocol, such as TCP/IP or Novell IPX/SPX is required. Each device communicating via a network protocol must have, in addition to a unique MAC address, a unique network address. TCP/IP provides an addressing scheme for billions of unique network addresses, although address allocation must be administered to avoid duplications and to guarantee proper routing of data.

2.1.4 Packetizing of Data

User data is sent across the network in discrete packets, or frames. A large graphics file, for example, must be divided into multiple small packets for transport across the network. Each packet contains a portion of the original file, as well as sequencing and source/destination addressing in a packet header. At the receiving end, the network-specific addressing and sequence information is removed and the data reassembled to recreate the original file.

2.1.5 Routing of Packets

Networks consist of multiple segments joined by routers or switches. Physical segmentation of a network is required to avoid overloading the transport with too many users and thus degrading performance. Users on a single shared LAN segment can communicate directly with one another. If a user wishes to communicate to someone on a different LAN segment, the data must be forwarded by a router or a switch. Managing the bandwidth available on a single segment and allocating sufficient router or switch ports for access to the rest of the network are fundamental challenges of network design.

In addition to getting packets across multiple segments, routing enables redundant links to be created between those segments. A **meshed network** refers to a topology that provides multiple data paths between its participants. If a single link goes down, the meshed network can route data around the failure and still get data to its final destination.

2.1.6 Upper-Layer Protocol Support

Network topologies and protocols provide the communications infrastructure for upper-layer applications. The network protocol layer is responsible only for moving data from one point to another. What is done with the data once it arrives is the responsibility of upper-layer protocols. IP, for example, routes packets through the network to the intended destination. Sitting above IP, the TCP (or similar layer) formats the data for hand-off to the application. SANs also support TCP/IP, but the dominant upper-layer protocol used in SANs is a SCSI variant protocol optimized for moving blocks of data to and from disk.

2.2 Traditional SCSI Bus Architecture

Until recently, network topologies terminated at the file server, or host computer. Remote and local users used network protocols and infrastructure to send or to retrieve data from the server, but the server itself used nonnetwork topologies to store and to retrieve data from disk and tape. The most common method for connecting disk and tape devices to the server has been the SCSI bus architecture.

SCSI is both a protocol and a physical transport. The SCSI protocol specifies controls and commands for sending blocks of data between disk and the file server. The operating system responds to a user's request for data, such as saving a document, by issuing the appropriate series of SCSI commands to the interface card that drives the disk array. Windows NT, for example, treats all disk and tape devices as SCSI devices. When a file is stored or retrieved from disk, a sequence of SCSI commands is launched to prepare the specified disk device for the read or write operation.

The original SCSI physical-layer transport was a parallel cable with 8 data lines and a number of control lines. Transmitting 8 bits of data during each transmit clock provides a relatively high bandwidth, but electrical issues restrict the total distance allowed by most SCSI implementations to 15–25 meters. The SCSI parallel bus architecture has evolved over time, with higher bandwidth provided by wider data paths (16 data lines and 32 data lines) and faster clocks.

One of the difficulties presented by a parallel bus architecture is a phenomenon known as **skew**. If 8 or 16 bits of data are sent simultaneously in parallel, small differences in propagation delay along each data line may occur, and all bits may not arrive at the destination at precisely the same moment. Skew refers to the window of time during which all data bits arrive at the target. The greater the differences in propagation delay, the wider the window must be to ensure that all data bits are captured. With a faster transmission clock, the cable length must be reduced to minimize skew.

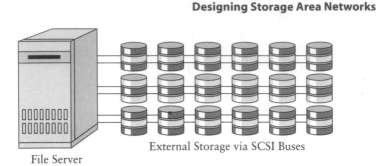

File Server   External Storage via SCSI Buses

Figure 2-5 *Server with multiple SCSI HBAs*

Additionally, parallel SCSI requires termination of any unused ports. As multiple SCSI devices are daisy chained together, end devices must be terminated to avoid erratic signal interference. Proper cabling and termination are critical for stable parallel SCSI operation. Marginal components or improper termination can cause data corruption or transaction failures.

File servers may house disk drives internally and provide either parallel SCSI cabling or a parallel SCSI backplane for installing disks. Current data requirements for most enterprises, however, make internal storage impractical.

To accommodate hundreds of gigabytes or terabytes of data, it is necessary to deploy multiple external disk enclosures, typically connected by parallel SCSI cabling to multiple SCSI host bus adapters (HBAs) installed in the server, as shown in Figure 2-5.

The movement of data from internal storage to external storage has been a driving force in finding alternative solutions to parallel SCSI architecture. Since no more than 15 storage arrays can be daisy chained together, a server system requiring terabytes of data would require multiple SCSI HBAs and multiple strings of disk enclosures. The sheer number of parallel cables required, the overall distance limitation of 15–25 meters, and the ensuring of the proper termination of each string pushes parallel SCSI architecture to its limits. If a particular disk array requires servicing or reconfiguration, the entire string of storage must be taken off line. For today's high-availability networks, this complexity and down time are often unacceptable.

2.3 Network-Attached Storage

One solution to parallel SCSI involves the removal of storage from behind the server and its reassignment to the messaging network or LAN in front of the server. In the process, the storage array must now be front-ended with a controller card that provides a LAN interface, LAN protocol support, and logic optimized for file access. The server, which previously was configured with both SCSI and LAN adapters, now requires only a LAN adapter for both storage and user communication.

Network-attached storage (NAS) resolves several problems associated with parallel SCSI buses and presents a few new ones. First, NAS eliminates the cumbersome configuration of SCSI HBAs, parallel cables, and termination normally associated with traditional SCSI server attachment. Second, NAS frees storage from its direct attachment to a particular server. If a storage array becomes a network-addressable device, any user or server running any operating system could, theoretically, access it via network protocols and a common file access protocol, such as Network File System (NFS). As illustrated in Figure 2-6, this universal access is the main benefit of NAS architecture. Third, if a storage array is completely offloaded from an individual server, it is conceivable to perform tape backups across the messaging network without consuming server resources.

Although these benefits overcome many of the shortcomings of parallel SCSI topologies, network-attached storage has a significant drawback. The bottleneck associated with storage transactions over parallel SCSI is now shifted onto the production network. The messaging network must now accommodate both end-user traffic and the users' and host systems' requests to disk. Even with switched 100Mbps Ethernet, it is difficult to deliver the bandwidth required for both.

In addition, the transaction overhead of SCSI protocol is now replaced with the additional protocol overhead required by the LAN. Wrapping packets of user data in UDP/IP (User Datagram Protocol/Internet Protocol) or TCP/IP may be acceptable for normal LAN and WAN transactions, but wrapping a disk access in UDP/IP or TCP/IP may contribute significantly to the total processing required. Ethernet, for example, has a maximum packet size of approximately

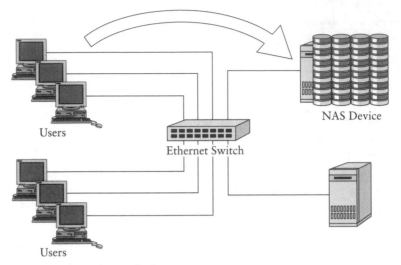

Figure 2-6 *Network-attached storage*

1,500 bytes. Reading a 5MB file from a network-attached storage device would require segmentation of the file into more than 3,500 individual packets of less than 1,500 bytes with either UDP/IP or TCP/IP header and trailer information for each packet. And since each packet must be issued individually by the LAN's access method, the protocol overhead is compounded by the LAN's data link requirements. Additional overhead is generated by NFS or similar file access protocols.

For these reasons, NAS is not normally implemented to solve bandwidth issues. Instead, NAS solves cross-platform and direct user access problems and removes data from the exclusive ownership of a single server.

Replacing the file server as a front-end device to storage with an embedded, LAN-enabled controller still leaves the issue of how the controller talks to disk. Some NAS solutions continue to use the SCSI bus architecture for disk arrays, whereas others use Fibre Channel. In the latter solutions, Fibre Channel is useful primarily for large populations of disks and redundancy.

Network-attached storage introduces the flexibility of networking to user and server/storage relations but potentially burdens the production network with traffic overload. This may be an acceptable trade-off if NAS devices are deployed primarily to accommodate heterogeneous operating systems and direct user access to disk.

Although NAS devices are a convenient technology for many network applications, they lack a SAN's ability to separate the server/storage network from the messaging network completely. NAS and SANs therefore fulfill different needs and may productively coexist within the same enterprise.

2.4 Networking behind the Server

Storage area networking (SAN) is predicated on the replacement of parallel SCSI transport with networked storage and tape *behind* the server (see Figure 2-7). SANs represent, after WANs and LANs, a third type of network, isolated from the messaging network and optimized for the movement of data from server to disk and tape.

Like network-attached storage, SANs rely on networking concepts and components to move files to and from disk. Unlike NAS devices, SANs are built on a separate network topology and, for the most part, do not rely on LAN protocols. The vast majority of SANs use Fibre Channel for the underlying network transport and, at the upper layer, move data to and from disks with serial SCSI (SCSI-3) protocol.

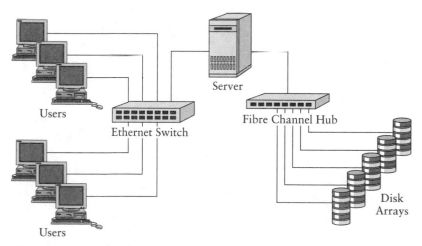

Figure 2-7 *A simple storage area network*

The combination of a high-speed transport with native SCSI protocol results in an efficient means to deploy servers, disk arrays, and tape subsystems and frees all components from the constraints of parallel SCSI architecture. Fibre Channel SANs provide high bandwidth (100MBps), long distances (to 10 km), and allow thousands of devices to exist on the same network. At the same time, SANs leverage the reliability of the SCSI protocol for moving disk data and facilitate new technologies (server clustering, storage clustering, LAN-free tape backup) that would be at best very awkward to accomplish with traditional parallel SCSI methods.

2.5 Summary

Networking in Front of the Server

- SANs bring new networking concepts to the server/storage model.

- Moving data serially allows higher speeds and longer distances between servers and storage.

- Access to the physical transport involves low-level protocols to ensure data integrity.

- Network addressing is required to identify each participant uniquely and to route data properly across the infrastructure.

- Large blocks of data must be segmented into packets, or frames, for orderly shipment through the network.

- Routing of data packets between network segments is performed by routers and switches.

- Networking facilitates movement of data whose source and destination are ultimately upper-level application interfaces. For SANs, the SCSI protocol rides over the Fibre Channel infrastructure to move blocks of data to and from disk.

Traditional SCSI Bus Architecture

- SCSI is both a protocol and a physical transport.

- Parallel SCSI architecture is limited by distance and the number of attached devices.

- Parallel SCSI configurations typically connect a single server to one or more disks.

Network-Attached Storage

- NAS moves storage from behind the server and places it on the production (Ethernet) network.

- NAS enables cross-platform access to common data but consumes network bandwidth.

- Vendors of NAS products may use Fibre Channel as a back-end architecture for higher-speed access to disks.

Networking behind the Server

- SANs are a separate network dedicated to storage.

- The majority of SANs use Fibre Channel as a transport and serial SCSI protocol to move data to and from disk.

- SANs enable new storage models, such as server clustering and LAN-free tape backup.

Fibre Channel Internals

3.1 Fibre Channel Layers

Fibre Channel is a standards-based networking architecture. Its standards provide definitions for physical-layer attributes, transport controls, and upper-level interfaces to TCP/IP, SCSI-3, HiPPI (High-Performance Parallel Interface), and other protocols. Fibre Channel is a gigabit transport, with current implementations at 1.0625 gigabaud. The ANSI (American National Standards Institute) T11X3 committee is the governing body for Fibre Channel standards. Resources for the various Fibre Channel documents are listed in Appendix B.

Fibre Channel standards define a multilayered architecture for moving data across the network. As listed in Table 3-1, these layers are numbered from FC-1 to FC-4. The top layer, FC-4, establishes the interface between Fibre Channel and upper-level applications. The serial SCSI protocol, for example, must map Fibre Channel devices to logical drives that can be accessed by the operating system. For host bus adapters, this function is typically fulfilled by the device driver provided by the vendor. FC-3 is under development and may include facilities for data encryption and compression. The FC-2 layer defines how blocks of data handed down by the upper-level application will be segmented into sequences of frames for hand-off to the transport layers. This layer also includes various classes of services and flow control mechanisms. The lower two layers, FC-1 and FC-0, focus on the transport of data across the network. FC-1 provides facilities for encoding and decoding data for shipment at gigabit speeds and defines the

Table 3-1	Fibre Channel Layers	
Layer	Function	Example of Use
FC-4	Upper-layer protocol interface	SCSI-3, IP, SBCCS (Single-Byte Command Code Set Mapping)
FC-3	Common services	Under construction
FC-2	Data delivery	Framing, flow control, service class
FC-1	Ordered sets/byte encoding	8b/10b encoding, link controls
FC-0	Physical interface	Optical/electrical, cable plant

command structure for accessing the media. FC-0 establishes standards for various media types, allowable lengths, and signaling.

This layered architecture is implemented on three transport topologies: point to point, Arbitrated Loop, and switched fabric. Point to point is a dedicated connection between two devices only, typically a server and a disk. Arbitrated Loop is a shared media, similar to Token Ring or FDDI (Fiber Distributed Data Interface), and uses a special superset of commands to control access to the media by multiple devices. A Fibre Channel fabric is one or more switches providing higher-level services and switched 100MBps bandwidth per port. Each of these topologies is discussed in detail in Chapter 4.

3.2 Gigabit Transport

To move data bits with integrity over a physical medium, a reference clock must be provided to ensure that each bit is received as it was transmitted. In parallel topologies, this function is served by a separate clock, or strobe line. As data bits are launched in parallel from the source, the strobe line toggles high or low to signal the receiving end that a full byte—or multiple bytes for 16- and 32-bit wide parallel cabling—has been sent.

Since serial data transports may have only two leads (transmit and receive), clocking cannot be achieved by a separate line. The serial data itself must carry the reference timing; that is, clocking must be embedded in the bit stream. Serial transports accomplish embedded clocking by various means. Fibre Channel uses a byte-encoding scheme and CDR (clock and data recovery) circuitry to recover clock and thus determine the data bits that comprise bytes and words.

At gigabit speeds, maintaining valid signaling—and therefore valid data recovery—is critical for data integrity. Fibre Channel standards allow for a single bit error to occur only once in a trillion bits (10^{-12}). In practice, this amounts to a maximum of one bit error every 16 minutes, although actual occurrence is far less frequent. One of the challenges for Fibre Channel vendors is to improve on this bit error rate. Reducing the rate to 10^{-13} would reduce statistical occurrence to one bit error every 2½ hours. Such reductions are possible if attention is given to the hardware interface design, cable quality, cable length, and the system **jitter budget.**

Jitter refers to any deviation in timing that a bit stream suffers as it traverses the physical medium and the circuitry on-board the end devices. A certain amount of deviation from the original signaling will naturally occur as a serial bit stream propagates over fiber-optic or copper cabling. Signaling may also be affected by transients from power supplies, board design, and other sources of electromagnetic interference (EMI). Recognizing that jitter cannot be completely eliminated, Fibre Channel standards have attempted to set guidelines for how much jitter individual components may contribute. If each product abides by the recommended jitter budget, timing deviations to gigabit signaling with a system should not exceed the recommended bit error rate of 10^{-12}.

Measuring the jitter contribution of any component requires expertise and expensive equipment. Since test equipment itself may contribute to jitter, research for better techniques and test facilities is ongoing. The ANSI T11.2 Methodologies for Jitter Specification group (MJS) is one official body that is attempting to define valid, nonintrusive methods for measuring and defining jitter limits.

Jitter is typically represented in graphical form by an "eye" diagram on a test scope, as illustrated in Figure 3-1. The cross-over points, or intersections forming the eye, represent signaling transitions to high or low voltages. Ideally, all transitions should occur at precisely the same interval. If that were the case, the clock and data recovery circuitry could recover all data bits, with no bit errors whatsoever. In reality, some deviation will always be observed. If the jitter is too extreme,

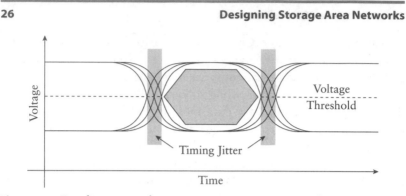

Figure 3-1 *Eye diagram, with transitions in eye representing bit errors*

the CDR will miss one or several bits, resulting in the corruption of Fibre Channel words or data within frames.

Jitter is an important element in SAN design, since every component may potentially contribute to jitter or jitter accumulation. A faulty transceiver, substandard fiber-optic cabling or connectors, exceeded cable distance guidelines, improperly shielded copper components, or simply bad product design can introduce system instability at the physical layer. Despite the marketing material of some vendors, no Fibre Channel product is jitter-free. Consequently, selection of low-jitter components should be based, where possible, on independent verification, such as Medusa Labs, in addition to the vendor's product specification.

3.3 Physical-Layer Options

Fibre Channel may be run over optical or copper media. Due to its noise immunity, fiber-optic cabling is preferred, but copper is also widely used, particularly for small form-factor Fibre Channel disk drives. Mixing fiber-optic and copper components in the same environment is supported, although not all products provide that flexibility.

For Fibre Channel transport, copper cabling is typically twinaxial and is specified as either **intracabinet** or **intercabinet**. Intracabinet copper assumes that all connections will be made within a single enclosure, such as a 19-inch rack. This reduces exposure to EMI and potential

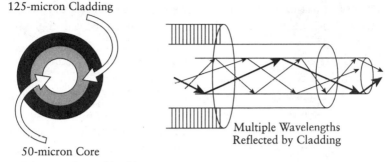

125-micron Cladding

50-micron Core

Multiple Wavelengths
Reflected by Cladding

Figure 3-2 *Multimode cabling*

ground loop problems. Intracabinet copper uses unequalized cabling to distances of 13 meters. Intercabinet copper requires active components on the signal-generation circuitry to reduce EMI and to drive the signal longer distances. Intercabinet copper also requires equalized, or balanced, cabling to extend up to the maximum of 30 meters.

Fiber-optic cabling is normally referred to by **mode**, or the frequencies of light waves that are carried by a particular cable type. Multimode cabling is used with shortwave laser light and has either a 50 micron or a 62.5-micron core with 125-micron cladding. The reflective cladding around the core restricts light to the core. The 50- or 62.5-micron diameter is sufficiently large for injected light waves to be reflected off the core interior, as shown in Figure 3-2. Since a shortwave laser beam comprises hundreds of light modes that will reflect off the core at different angles, a dispersion effect reduces the total distance at which the original signal can be reclaimed. Multimode fiber supports 175 meters with 62.5-micron/125-micron cable, and 500 meters with 50-micron/125-micron cable.

Single-mode fiber is constructed with a 9-micron core and 125-micron cladding. Single mode is used to carry longwave laser light. With a much smaller diameter core and a single-mode light source, single-mode fiber supports much longer distances, currently up to 10 km at gigabit speeds.

Both optic cable types are protected by an exterior coating, usually in a distinctive orange color, and use standard (SC) fiber-optic connectors for attachment to transceivers. The bend radius for fiber-optic cable should not exceed 3 inches, so some attention should be given to strain relief at connection points and routing of cabling within cabinets.

The selection of copper or optical media is determined by a number of practical considerations. Copper may present EMI issues but is sometimes mandated by other concerns. Some Fibre Channel products provide only copper DB-9 interfaces. Copper adapters are also less expensive than fiber-optic ones, which drives copper into price-sensitive configurations. Fiber-optic components and cabling, however, eliminate most of the EMI and ground loop problems that may occur with copper and are the preferred media for stable SAN construction.

At either end of the cable plant, transceivers or adapters are used to bring the gigabit bit stream onto the circuit boards of host bus adapters or controller cards. A number of form factors and interface types are available for both copper and optical media. For copper, this connection is fairly straightforward: electrical in (for example, from the copper cable plant), electrical out (for example, onto the copper traces of the controller's circuit board). For optical media, the optical pulses must be converted to electrical, that is, copper, and vice versa. Fiber-optic transceivers fulfill this role.

One of the first adapters developed for Fibre Channel applications was the gigabaud link module, or GLM. GLMs are available in both fiber-optic and copper versions, although their popularity has declined as new form factors have emerged. GLMs are semipermanent modules. A connector latches the GLM onto the circuit board of the HBA or controller, and the circuit board, in turn, is enclosed in a server chassis, disk cabinet, switch, or hub. Maintenance is an issue with GLMs, since the enclosure must be powered off and opened to replace or to reseat the module.

From a product design standpoint, GLMs saved the HBA or controller architect several design steps by incorporating, in addition to the optical or copper interface, clock and data recovery components, and serializing/deserializing circuitry. The connection between the GLM and its host card is a parallel interface. Encoded bytes can be sent or received via the connector with no additional parallel/serial conversion. In the end, this convenience for the architect has been outweighed by the inconvenience GLMs pose for maintenance and replacement.

The most widely used transceiver module for Fibre Channel is the gigabit interface converter, or GBIC. The GBIC form factor was first developed by Compaq, Sun, Amp, and Vixel Corporation and has become a de facto standard in the industry. GBICs lack the serializing/deserializing capability of GLMs but are modular, hot-swappable devices. This allows GBICs to be inserted or removed without powering down or opening the supporting chassis and facilitates replacement of one media with another, such as a copper GBIC with an optical GBIC. GBIC-based Fibre Channel switches and hubs offer greater flexibility in SAN design, primarily through the ability to mix various media and interface types and to make changes to the topology with less disruption to the system.

Optical GBICs are available in both shortwave (to 500 m) and longwave (to 10 km) versions and have standard dual SC connectors for attaching cabling. Copper GBICs are available in passive (to 13 m) and active (to 30 m) versions and use DB-9 or HSSDC (high-speed serial direct connect) cable interfaces. The HSSDC interface was developed by Amp and provides quicker cable attachment/removal compared to the lock-down screw design of the DB-9 connector.

The GBIC specification assigns module definition (mod-def) pins on the 20 pin connector. Signals on these pins indicate the GBIC type and can be read by the supporting HBA or controller circuitry. Appendix D of the specification also defines a voluntary serial ID function that, if supported by the GBIC, would allow a supporting device to read additional information from memory on-board the GBIC. Serial ID establishes fixed data fields for inventory information (manufacturer, model number, serial number, media supported, and so on) and vendor-assignable data fields for other useful information. The trend in GBIC design is toward more value-added use of serial ID, including on-board diagnostics and power/temperature reporting. To be useful, this information must be queried and interpreted by supporting logic in the host HBA, controller, switch, or hub and reported to management software.

A third transceiver device, the "1×9" form factor, is a fixed-function optical transceiver that is permanently mounted on the host system card. This module is less expensive than either optical GLMs or GBICs but lacks flexibility in mixing media types or interfaces. In the case of a Fibre Channel switch or hub based on "1×9" components, the failure of a single port assumes that the entire product is a field-replaceable unit (FRU).

If a SAN design requires an all-optical solution, copper-only devices can be accommodated with media interface adapters, or MIAs. MIAs typically provide a DB-9 connector on one end and a dual SC optical connector on the other. Power to drive the MIA's transceiver function may be drawn through the DB-9 connector—if the supporting electronics supply power and ground pins—or via an AC adapter. MIAs introduce an additional component, and therefore another potential point of failure, into the topology but are a viable means to overcome copper EMI and distance limitations.

Since fiber optics pose a potential laser safety issue, early implementations used an **open fiber control (OFC)** mechanism to shut down laser transmission when a cable was removed or broken. The OFC feature is based on a signaling handshake between two devices. If a receiver loses signal, it initially shuts off its transmitter and then begins a series of low-intensity signals to its partner. If the partner also responds with low-intensity signals (for example, the cable is re-attached), both sides boost their laser output to resume normal activity. The time required to complete OFC handshake is unsuited to some topologies, particularly Arbitrated Loop. The development of new laser technology that could support full-speed signaling at safer, low intensities has resulted in a class of GLMs and GBICs known as **non-OFC** transceivers. Currently, most transceivers used for SANs are based on the non-OFC standard. Still, it is not advisable to stare directly into any laser source.

3.4 Data Encoding

Proper transmission and reception of a digital bit stream would not be possible if raw bytes of data were simply herded into a shift register and shoved one bit at a time onto the transport. Among all the possible combinations of 1s and 0s in an 8-bit byte, and the possible combinations of bytes that could be sent one after the other, bit streams with sustained 1s or 0s could occur. A raw stream of hex FF (binary 1111 1111) bytes would, for example, appear as a sustained DC positive voltage on the transmission line. Without a byte-encoding scheme to force transitions from positive to negative, it would be impossible to detect when one bit ended and another began; that is, it would be impossible to recover the clocking used to issue the stream.

This problem is exacerbated at gigabit speeds. At over a thousand million bits per second and a standards-enforced bit error rate of 10^{-12}, the Fibre Channel physical transport must ensure that every bit is properly recovered for reassembly into valid bytes. This is accomplished with an efficient encoding scheme that ensures that no sustained highs or lows will occur in the transport signal.

First developed by IBM, the 8b/10b encoding algorithm depicted in Figure 3-3 converts each 8-bit byte into two possible 10-bit characters. Each of the two 10-bit products of this conversion should have no more than six total 1s or 0s; about half will have an equal number of 1s and 0s. The 10-bit characters with more 1s than 0s have **positive disparity**, whereas those with more 0s than 1s have **negative disparity**. An even balance of 1s and 0s results in **neutral disparity**.

In processing all 256 possible data bytes, the 8b/10b mechanism allows only the maximum of 6 bits of the same type per character, with no more than four of the same bit type to occur sequentially. The hex byte x'FF', for example, is encoded from its original binary 1111 1111 into either 101011 0001 or 010100 1110. Both products have neutral disparity, and neither has more than four of the same bit type in sequence.

Within the possible combinations that can be generated with 10 bits, some have no relation to the standard 256 data bytes. Fibre Channel uses one of these nondata characters as a special command character. Known as the K28.5 command character, it has a positive disparity

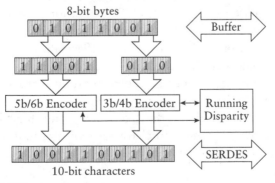

Figure 3-3 *8b/10b encoding logic*

composition as 001111 1010 and a negative disparity as 110000 0101. In both instances, the special character has 2 bits of one type followed by 5 bits of the opposite, which immediately distinguishes the command character from ordinary encoded data characters. This unique "comma" sequence is used by data-recovery circuitry as a trigger for defining the boundaries of 10-bit characters. Once the comma sequence is detected in a serial bit stream, data recovery can begin picking up entire characters simply by counting the bits to the beginning of the next 10-bit character.

Since the conversion of 8-bit data bytes results in two 10-bit results, how does the 8b/10b encoder decide which result to use? If the choice were arbitrary, the sequential shipment of some 10-bit characters would, in combination, result in an imbalance of the same bit types—including instances of 5 bits in sequence—appearing on the bit stream. The clock and data recovery circuitry at the receiving end would then be unable to retrieve valid characters.

The 8b/10b encoder resolves this problem by monitoring the disparity of the previously processed character. If a positive-disparity character is transmitted, the next character issued should have negative disparity. By monitoring the **running disparity** of the previous event, the encoder can ensure that an overall balance of 1s and 0s is maintained in the serial stream. Data bytes that encode to two equally balanced results—equal number of 1s and 0s—have one result that is used when the current running disparity is positive and another when the current running disparity is negative.

The 8b/10b notation is expressed in dotted-decimal subsets of the original data byte before it undergoes encoding. A hex xD7, for example, has a bit pattern of 1101 0111. The notation scheme divides this pattern into the first 3 bits: 110 (decimal 6), followed by the byte's last 5 bits, 10111 (decimal 23). This division reflects the internal operation of the 8b/10b encoder, since these units are processed in smaller 3b/4b and 5b/6b modules and then swapped to produce the 10-bit results. Consequently, 8b/10b notation refers to xD7 as D23.6. The only intuitive aspect of this notation is the "D," which stands for "data." The K in the unique K28.5 command character indicates that it is a special character. It is distinguished from D28.5 (xBC) by virtue of its exclusive comma sequence.

The practical impact of 8b/10b encoding on general SAN design becomes clear when we examine Fibre Channel protocol, addressing, and hardware issues. For all the effort to maintain a more even distribution of 1s and 0s in the gigabit stream, some quite valid sequences of encoded characters nonetheless stress the ability of the recovery circuitry to capture data. The 8b/10b algorithm is also responsible for the address space allocated to Arbitrated Loop, as discussed later.

3.5 Ordered Sets

To move data across the network, Fibre Channel uses a concise command syntax referred to as **ordered sets**. These transmission words comprise 4 encoded bytes, or 40 bits, the first byte of which is the K28.5 special character. Ordered set recognition logic triggers on the K28.5 character, and the three following data bytes define what function the ordered set provides.

Ordered sets fall into three general categories. One subset is used to indicate the start and end of data frames and the class of service used to ship the frame. The start-of-frame delimiter K28.5 D21.5 D22.2 D22.2, for example, is used as a frame header to initiate a connectionless level of service. Following the start-of-frame ordered set, up to 2,112 bytes of data would comprise the body of the frame. An end-of-frame ordered set, such as K28.5 D21.4 D21.6 D21.6, would indicate that the transmission of this frame was complete. Fibre Channel defines 11 types of start-of-frame (SOF) ordered sets, and 8 end-of-frame (EOF) words. The specific SOF or EOF used informs the recipient as to what further action, such as an acknowledgment, if any, is required.

A group of ordered sets, known as **primitive signals**, is used to indicate actions or events on the transport. The IDLE primitive, for example, has the notation K28.5 D21.4 D21.5 D21.5 and is used as a fill word between data frames and during periods of inactivity. The Close primitive (CLS) is used in Arbitrated Loop configurations to indicate the end of a transaction. Only a single occurrence of a primitive signal is required to trigger a response. If a primitive signal is missed or is corrupted in transport—for example, by excessive jitter on a link—logic on the end nodes should time out on the transaction and recover via higher-level protocols.

Primitive sequences are ordered sets used to indicate or initiate state changes on the transport. Unlike primitive signals, primitive sequences require at least three consecutive words to be recognized before any action is taken. A Fibre Channel disk drive, for example, would issue a sequence of Loop Initialization primitives (LIPs) when first inserted into an Arbitrated Loop topology. Downstream nodes would not respond to the primitive sequence until three of the LIPs had been received.

Although most frame-delimiting ordered sets are common to all Fibre Channel topologies, supersets of primitive signals and primitive sequences have been defined specifically for Arbitrated Loop and Fibre Channel fabric. A shared topology, such as Arbitrated Loop, requires special commands for gaining exclusive control of the transport. A dedicated connection to a fabric, on the other hand, assumes that the transport is always available and so requires no negotiation for access. The ordered sets unique to each topology are discussed in Chapter 4.

3.6 Framing Protocol

To move data from one Fibre Channel–attached device to another, the data blocks handed down by the upper-layer protocol of the sender must be organized into discrete packets for shipment across the transport. In Fibre Channel nomenclature, data packets are referred to as **frames.**

Frames are always prefaced with an ordered set start-of-frame (SOF) delimiter. This single 4-byte word defines the class of service used and whether the frame is the first in a series or simply one of a series of related frames. Following the SOF, a 24-byte frame header contains destination and source addressing, as well as control fields that indicate the frame's content—control information or data type—and position within a series of sequential frames. After the header comes the data unit, which may be from 0 to 2,112 bytes. This variable-length data-framing technique allows Fibre Channel to accommodate various application requirements, with a reasonable balance between frame overhead and payload. Since Fibre Channel frame construction is based on multiples of 4-byte transmission words, the user data must be padded with additional fill bytes if the total byte count is not evenly divisible by 4. A 509-byte payload, for example, would need three additional fill bytes for proper frame assembly. Data integrity within the frame is verified with a 32-bit cyclic redundancy check (CRC). The CRC calculation is performed before the data is run through the 8b/10b encoder, and the 4-byte CRC itself is later encoded along with the rest of the frame contents. Following the CRC, an end-of-frame (EOF) ordered set is appended to notify the recipient that the frame is complete. The specific EOF used is determined by the class of service and whether the frame is one of or the last of a series of frames. The Fibre Channel frame format is as follows:

SOF	Header	Data Field	CRC	EOF

In addition to the standard 24-byte frame header, optional headers may be used for applications that require extensive control fields. To keep the total frame size within 2,148 bytes, the optional headers must occupy part of the 2,112-byte data space and so may reduce the data payload by as much as 64 bytes per frame. The presence of optional headers should be recognized when calculating data throughput in Fibre Channel environments. For most applications, it is sufficient simply to count the bytes between SOF and EOF and to deduct 28 bytes (normal header + CRC) to determine the data payload.

Once the frame is assembled, frame delivery is accomplished by a protocol hierarchy of **sequences** and **exchanges**. A sequence may include one or more related frames, such as a single file written to disk via multiple frames, whereas an exchange may include one or more unrelated sequences. Two communicating devices, in turn, may have several exchanges established at the same time, with unique exchange IDs and sequence IDs separating the traffic. This nested structure of exchanges and sequences of frames maximizes utilization of the link between two devices with minimal overhead for setting up and tearing down logical connections.

To further minimize overhead in frame transport, Fibre Channel limits error recovery to the sequence level. If a frame fails the CRC check, for example, it is more efficient to recover by reissuing the entire sequence of frames at gigabit speed than to embed the logic required to track and to recover individual frames.

3.7 Class of Service

Applications may require various levels of delivery guarantees, bandwidth, and connectivity between communicators to ensure proper data transport. Data streaming for a tape-backup application, for example, implies a sustained, dedicated connection and full-bandwidth availability. Alternatively, with intermittent activity, online transaction processing (OLTP) may not require dedicated bandwidth but would benefit from acknowledgments for each transfer. To accommodate these requirements, Fibre Channel standards provide five classes of service, although not all are implemented in real products.

Class 1 service defines a dedicated connection between two devices—for example, a file server and a disk array—with acknowledgment of frame delivery. The communicating partners establish a Class 1 connection and then assume full bandwidth and a constant circuit until the connection is taken down. Because the Class 1 circuit in most cases excludes others from intervening in the conversation, there is no danger that one of the partners will be busied out during an exchange. The dedicated connection also ensures that all frames will be received in the same order they were sent, which speeds reassembly of data blocks at the FC-2 level.

Class 1 service places an additional design burden on the Fibre Channel switches. A Class 1 connection between a server and a disk that are communicating via a switch consumes switch-routing resources. The switch must maintain a dedicated 100MBps channel between the communicating ports and is not allowed to intervene in any way. Multiple Class 1 connections by multiple pairs would thus quickly impede the switch's ability to service other requests to those ports. Analogous to a phone switch, Class 1 service provides a clamp-on facility that, if supported by the switch, allows a contending request to be queued against a busy port. As soon as the current Class 1 connection is ended, the new request can be serviced. This requires additional buffering on the switch and logic to monitor the queue and time-out values. Class 1 service also defines a stacked connect feature that allows a Class 1 participant to queue additional connect requests to the switch. Due to the added complexity and cost associated with

Class 1 functionality, these features are not widely implemented by Fibre Channel switch vendors.

Class 1 service may also be implemented in a nonswitched topology, such as Arbitrated Loop. Typically, however, loop implementations use the more democratic Class 3 service.

Class 2 service does not require a dedicated connection between talking pairs but does provide acknowledgment of frame delivery. In switch environments, the connectionless nature of Class 2 allows the switch to forward frames as resources allow without dedicating bandwidth to a transaction. Traffic congestion or multiple routes may therefore result in frames being received in a random order, which would require additional processing overhead for reassembly into data blocks. To alleviate this possibility, a Class 2 connection may request in-order delivery. In Arbitrated Loop environments, a Class 2 transfer ensures in-order delivery of frames, since only the communicating partners occupy the loop for the duration of the transaction.

Class 2 is suited to mission-critical applications that demand a high degree of data integrity at the transport level. Acknowledgment of frame delivery and notification of nondelivery adds an additional validation without involving upper-level protocols. Class 2 is also suited to smaller data transactions with only bursty traffic requirements. Intermittent updates to a relational database, for example, do not require a dedicated connection but may need verification via frame acknowledgments.

Class 3 service, like Class 2, is connectionless, but unlike Class 2, there is no notification of delivery. Class 3 is similar to datagram services in LAN topologies—for example, UDP/IP—and relies on upper-level protocols to recover if a transport error occurs. To a certain extent, Class 3 service sacrifices reliability for reduced overhead and higher performance. In well-constructed SANs, the reliability factor may not be a pressing issue. Class 3, for example, is widely used in Arbitrated Loop environments, even for mission-critical applications. This is possible due to the temporary dedicated connections between partners that a loop topology provides. Frames will be received in order and, with the selection of appropriate products, the low occurrence of bit errors results in reliable frame transport. In a heavily burdened switch topology, Class 3's inherent laissez-faire attitude toward frame delivery is more apparent. A switch may discard Class 3 frames under congested conditions and, since there is no acknowledgment mechanism, trigger a more lengthy recovery chain reaction at the FC-4 upper protocol level.

This difference between loop and switch Class 3 handling should be considered when designing SANs for specific applications. Some Class 3 implementations are more reliably deployed on loop segments alone, whereas others, depending on bandwidth allocation requirements, may be reasonably configured with a combination of loop segments and switch topologies.

For multiclass applications, Fibre Channel provides an optional intermix feature. Intermix allows any unused bandwidth in a Class 1 connection to be used by Class 2 and Class 3 frames. The operative descriptor is *unused,* since Class 1, by definition, guarantees full bandwidth when Class 1 frames are present. If implemented, intermix is useful for applications like tape backup, since Class 2 or 3 frames could be used to set up the next transaction while a Class 1 connection is still active.

Two additional classes of service have been defined, but are not widely implemented, for specialized applications. Class 4 service introduces the concept of virtual circuits to Fibre Channel architecture. Like Class 1, Class 4 service is connection-oriented. But instead of allocating the entire bandwidth between communicating pairs, Class 4 allows fractional bandwidth to be assigned, as well as different quality-of-service (QoS) parameters for each connection. Additionally, multiple virtual circuits may be established between a single pair or multiple pairs. The mandated quality of service for each virtual circuit ensures that time-sensitive applications, such as real-time video, always have bandwidth available for transmission. The functionality described by Class 4 service poses considerable design challenges to switch architects. The switch must maintain and monitor potentially hundreds of virtual circuits, with variable QoS parameters for each one. This complexity may explain why Class 4 capability exists primarily as a Fibre Channel standard and not as a standard feature of switch products.

Class 6 has been defined to provide multicast service with acknowledged delivery. Multicast is a requirement for video broadcast applications based on a central video server and multiple video recipients. This function can also be provided by Class 3 datagram service if acknowledgment is not required. Depending on the number of target devices in a multicast group, the number of acknowledgments flooding back to an initiator might overwhelm the topology. Class 6 alleviates this problem by placing a multicast server into the configuration. The multicast server is the focal point for all acknowledgments and, for each multicast transaction, returns a single confirmation to the initiator.

Although Class 4 and Class 6 services are sometimes described in granular detail in Fibre Channel literature, that does not mean that these features have been implemented in tangible products. Fibre Channel switches, for example, typically list support for Class 2 and Class 3 services only. Support for other functionality is driven, like everything else, by market demand. The fact that Class 4 and Class 6 have emerged as Fibre Channel standards, however, reflects not only the influence of market requirements on the technology but also that cooperation between customers and vendors is driving higher functionality into products.

3.8 Flow Control

To prevent a target device from being overwhelmed with frames, Fibre Channel provides several flow control mechanisms based on a system of credits. Each credit represents a device's ability to accept an additional frame. If no credits are issued by the recipient to the sender, no frames can be sent. Pacing frame transport on the basis of credits prevents loss of frames and reduces the frequency of entire sequences being retransmitted across the link.

In practice, this credit scheme is based on the number of buffers that an end node maintains for storing incoming data. Memory onboard a host bus adapter, for example, may be allocated as receive buffers to interface between the deserializing and decoding functions of FC-1 and the frame reassembly function of FC-2. The receive buffers are filled as frames are handed up by FC-1 and are emptied as FC-2's assembly line pulls individual frames for reconstruction into data blocks.

For efficient utilization of the Fibre Channel transport, it is useful if multiple frames can be sent consecutively. This is accomplished by granting sufficient credits before a transaction begins and by using

Fibre Channel's full-duplex capability to send additional credits while frames are still being received.

Transmission credit is initially established when two communicating nodes log in and exchange communication parameters. End-to-end flow control (EE_Credit) is used by Class 1 and Class 2 service between two end nodes and is monitored by the nodes themselves. An intervening switch does not participate in EE_Credit. Once an initial credit level is granted, the replenishment of credits is accomplished by acknowledgments issued by the receiver to the sender. The sender decrements the EE_Credit by 1 for each frame issued and increments only when an ACK is received.

Buffer-to-buffer credit (BB_Credit) is used by Class 2 and Class 3 service and relies on the receiver-ready (R_RDY) ordered set to replenish credits. An end node attached to a switch will establish its BB_Credit during login to the fabric. A communicating partner on the far side of the switch will establish its own (and possibly different) BB_Credit to the switch during login. BB_Credit thus has no end-to-end component. A sender decrements the BB_Credit by 1 for each frame sent and increments BB_Credit by 1 for each R_RDY received. The initial value of the BB_Credit must be nonzero.

In Arbitrated Loop, a different BB_Credit scheme is used. This BB_Credit assumes that the BB_Credit of a device is 0. The target node does not establish a positive BB_Credit until it is opened for a transaction by an initiator. The target then issues a number of R_RDYs equivalent to the receive buffers it has available. The differentiating feature of this BB_Credit is that an initiator does not have to maintain a table of BB_Credit values for potentially more than a hundred targets on the same loop. By simply setting the initial value to 0 and relying on R_RDYs to establish credit, the overhead on loop devices is dramatically reduced.

3.9 Name and Addressing Conventions

The unique identity of participants in a Fibre Channel environment is maintained through a hierarchy of fixed names and assigned address identifiers. In Fibre Channel terminology, a communicating device is a **node**. A host bus adapter in a server, for example, constitutes a Fibre Channel Node. Normally, the Node has only one physical interface, known as a Node Port or **N_Port**. If an HBA or a controller is multi-ported—some have as many as four physical ports per card—it is possible for a single node to have multiple N_Ports.

Each Node has a fixed 64-bit **Node_Name** assigned by the manufacturer. If the manufacturer has registered for a range of addresses with the IEEE, the Node Name will be globally unique and so is normally referred to as a **World-Wide Name**. An N_Port within a parent node is also assigned a unique 64-bit **Port_Name**, which typically follows the IEEE format. This naming convention allows each node and its associated N_Ports to be unique and accessible, even in complex SANs. Standards allow for several IEEE formats, as well as 64-bit formats for IP and locally administered names.

Similar to the 48-bit MAC address scheme in Ethernet and Token Ring, the Fibre Channel naming convention allows either global or locally administered uniqueness to be assigned to a device. Unlike the LAN MAC address, however, the administered Name or World-Wide Name is not used for transporting frames across the network. In addition to a Fibre Channel Name, a communicating device is dynamically assigned a 24-bit **port address**, or **N_Port ID** that is used for frame routing (see Figure 3-4). The 24-bit addresses of two communicating partners are embedded in the frame header for both the destination identifier (D_ID) and source identifier (S_ID).

This dual Name and Address system has several benefits. The 64-bit name provides a unique identity throughout the SAN. Using 64-bit identifiers for routing data, however, would fatten the frame header and incur more processing overhead. By using a shorter, 24-bit port address, the frame header and the routing logic are optimized for high-speed switching of frames. The 24-bit format still allows for more than 16 million addresses, an address space far larger than any practical SAN design. (Of course, that was the view of the original Internet IP address space as well.)

In addition to optimizing frame routing, the 24-bit port address strategy removes manual administration of addresses by allowing the topology itself to assign addresses. In fabric environments, the switch is responsible for assigning a 24-bit address to each device as it logs on. The switch maintains a table of the device's World-Wide Name and the assigned 24-bit address in the Simple Name Server. In Arbitrated Loop, the loop devices themselves perform an address selection routine,

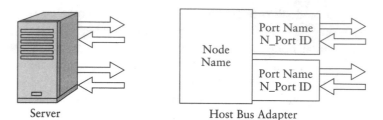

Figure 3-4 *Server with a dual-ported host bus adapter*

which ensures that every device on the loop has a unique address. Dynamic addressing removes the element of human error in address maintenance and provides more flexibility in adds, moves, and changes in the SAN.

An N_Port may be attached directly to another N_Port, as in a point-to-point topology. In a fabric, the N_Port is attached to a fabric port, or **F_Port**. Each switch port also has a 64-bit Port_Name, and the switch itself, like a Node, has a 64-bit Fabric_Name. The unique identity of each switch and switch port, as well as each attached node port, is thus established for the entire SAN.

Connections between fabric switches are maintained by expansion ports, or **E_Ports**. If the switch vendor provides ports that can be used for either node attachment or expansion, a generic port, or **G_Port**, definition is used. Finally, a switch may also allow attachment of public Arbitrated Loop devices on Fabric Loop Ports, or **FL_Ports**. The attached Arbitrated Loop ports are referred to as Node Loop Ports, or **NL_Ports**. The NL_Port/FL_Port connection requires higher functionality and protocol support on the part of the NL_Port, including log-on facilities and registration with the switch's Simple Name Server. These fabric services may also be provided by a special NL_Port if no switch is present. This special port is defined as a Fabric/Node Loop Port, or **F/NL_Port**.

A free-standing Arbitrated Loop is configured with multiple NL_Ports on a shared media. If the NL_Ports are connected through an Arbitrated Loop hub, the hub plays no active role in frame routing decisions. Hub ports, therefore, have no particular designation, since the hub's existence is transparent to the attached devices. The trend in hub design is toward more intelligence, particularly for loop management and automatic-recovery features. If a vendor engineers a Fibre Channel controller in the hub architecture, it appears as an additional NL_Port to the topology.

3.10 Summary

FC Layers

- Fibre Channel is a standards-based, layered architecture.

- FC-0 defines the physical interface, which may be optical or copper.

- FC-1 provides low-level link controls and data encoding for gigabit transport.

- FC-2 defines segmentation and reassembly of data via frames, flow control, and classes of service.

- FC-3 is being developed for common services.

- FC-4 is the upper-layer protocol (ULP) interface between Fibre Channel and IP, SCSI-3, and other protocols.

Gigabit Transport

- Fibre Channel standards enforce a 10^{-12} bit error rate.

- Timing deviation is referred to as jitter. Fibre Channel network components are assigned a jitter budget; if the budget is exceeded, excessive errors may occur.

Physical-Layer Options

- Fibre Channel supports both optical and copper media.

- The maximum distance for intracabinet copper is 13 meters.

- The maximum distance for intercabinet copper is 30 meters.

- Shortwave laser supports up to 500 meters on 50-micron/125-micron multimode cable.

- Longwave laser supports up to 10 kilometers on 9-micron/125-micron single-mode cable.

- Transceiver modules include GLMs, GBICs, and 1x9s.

Data Encoding

- For reliable transport at gigabit speeds, data must be encoded.

- The 8b/10b encoding converts 8-bit bytes into 10-bit characters.

- The special K28.5 character is used to indicate Fibre Channel commands.

- Running disparity is used to maintain balanced signaling.

Ordered Sets

- A Fibre Channel word is four 10-bit characters.

- Words with K28.5 in the first character position are ordered sets.

- Ordered sets are used as frame delimiters, primitive signals, and primitive sequences for low-level transport protocol.

Framing Protocol

- Data is segmented into frames for transport.

- The maximum frame size is 2,148 bytes, with 2,112 bytes of payload.

- Frames are transmitted as sequences of related frames.

- An exchange may include multiple sequences.

Class of Service

- Class 1 service is a dedicated connection between two communicators with acknowledgment of frame delivery.

- Class 2 service is connectionless but provides acknowledgment.

- Class 3 service is connectionless and provides no notification of delivery.

- Class 4 allows fractional bandwidth for virtual circuits.

- Class 6 provides multicast with acknowledgment.

Flow Control

- Flow control is maintained by a credit scheme between communicators and prevents a target from being overwhelmed with frames.

- End-to-end credit is monitored by the communicating nodes and is replenished by acknowledgments.

- Buffer-to-buffer credit is replenished by receiver-ready primitives.

- An alternative buffer-to-buffer credit is used by Arbitrated Loop.

Name and Addressing Conventions

- A node is a communicating device.

- A node is identified by a unique 8-byte Node Name, or World-Wide Name.

- A node may contain multiple ports, or N_Ports, each of which has a unique 8-byte Port_Name.

- Each N_Port has a 24-bit port address, or N_Port ID, used for frame routing.

- A Fibre Channel fabric switch port is an F_Port for attachment to N_Ports, or an FL_Port when attached to Arbitrated Loop FL_Ports.

- An E_Port is a fabric switch expansion port used to connect fabrics.

SAN Topologies

Fibre Channel architecture has evolved three distinct physical topologies. The first SANs were built on a dedicated, point-to-point connection between two devices. Participants in a point-to-point topology establish an initial connection via login and then assume full-bandwidth availability. Arbitrated Loop allows more than two devices to communicate over a shared bandwidth. An initiator in a loop environment must negotiate for access to the media before launching a transaction. A Fibre Channel fabric topology provides multiple, concurrent, point-to-point connections via link-level switching and so entails a much higher level of complexity, both in the physical configuration and in transport protocol.

Depending on application requirements, all three topologies may be viable for SAN design. Although point-to-point configurations are more restrictive, Arbitrated Loop and fabrics offer a wide range of solutions for a variety of application needs. By incorporating application-specific integrated circuits (ASICs), switch and loop hub prices have declined while functionality has increased. And by providing attachment of loop topologies to fabric ports, it is now possible to design and implement complex SANs that efficiently service multiple, sometimes contending, applications. This was not the case just a few years ago.

4.1 Point to Point

A point-to-point topology is a simple, direct connection between two N_Ports. As shown in Figure 4-1, the transmit lead of one N_Port is

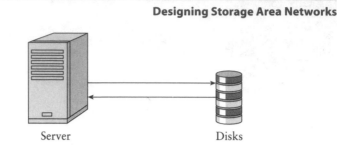

Server   Disks

Figure 4-1 *A point-to-point link between a server and a disk*

connected via copper or optical cabling to the receive lead of its partner. The partner's transmit, in turn, is cabled to the other N_Port's
receive lead. This cabling scheme creates dedicated bandwidth between
the pair, typically 100MBps in each direction.

Before data transactions can occur, the two N_Ports must perform
an N_Port login to assign N_Port addresses, or N_Port IDs. Thereafter,
a persistent connection is maintained, with utilization of the dedicated
link determined by the application.

Although it is conceivable to have an application requiring simultaneous full-duplex transfers, that is, 200MBps total throughput, in
practice only one side of the link sees any real traffic at a given
moment. A server and a disk in a point-to-point configuration would
normally be performing either reads or writes of data but not both
concurrently. From the server's standpoint, an ongoing read operation
would initiate incoming frames on the server's receiver, with only ACKs
(for Class 1 or 2 service) leaving the server's transmitter. Even then, the
100MBps available bandwidth on the server's receive link is not likely
to saturate. Link utilization in point-to-point configurations is determined by the performance of the Fibre Channel controllers at either
end and the buffering available to queue up data to be transmitted or
received.

The original point-to-point configurations were based on quarter-
speed, 266Mbps, bandwidth, with an effective throughput of 25MBps.
Distributed primarily by Sun Microsystems, quarter-speed implementations used fiber-optic GLMs as the transceiver interface to the
host bus adapter and disk controller logic. Tens of thousands of these
systems have been shipped to customers over the past several years,
creating a large but unadvertised base of Fibre Channel products in

production environments. This legacy base has provided valuable experience for improving both the physical transport and protocol support.

As server and disk performance have increased, Fibre Channel throughput has superseded quarter and half speed and now provides full gigabit bandwidth. At the same time, advances in fabric and Arbitrated Loop technology have enabled more flexibility and functionality than point to point provides. A point-to-point configuration is still viable for simple configurations; for growth of the SAN, however, it is important to select the proper HBA and controller components. If the vendor includes device drivers or microcode for both point-to-point protocol and Arbitrated Loop, accommodating additional devices on the SAN can be accomplished with minimal pain.

4.2 Arbitrated Loop

Arbitrated Loop is the most commonly deployed topology for Fibre Channel SANs. Loops provide more flexibility and support for more devices than does point to point and are more economical per port than are fabric switches. Loop-capable HBAs, Fibre Channel disks, and Fibre Channel–to–SCSI bridges are also more prevalent than fabric-capable devices, primarily because most of these devices have already passed through a development and interoperability cycle and have emerged as more stable products.

Arbitrated Loop is a shared, gigabit transport. Like shared Ethernet or Token Ring segments, the functional bandwidth available to any individual loop device is determined by the total population on the segment and the level of activity of the other participants: more active talkers, less available bandwidth. An Arbitrated Loop with 50 equally active nodes, for example, would provide 100MBps/50, or only 2MBps functional bandwidth per node. Arbitrated Loop would therefore not be a popular choice for SANs were it not for the fact that a typical storage network has relatively few active contenders for bandwidth. Although a single loop may have more than a hundred disk drives, there are usually no more than four to six servers initiating requests to those drives. Large configurations are thus possible on a single loop without dividing the bandwidth down to the level of ordinary Ethernet.

Since the transport is shared, some means must be provided for orderly access to the media. In Arbitrated Loop, media access is gained through an arbitration protocol. Once an NL_Port has arbitrated and won control of the transport, it has the full 100MBps bandwidth available for its transaction. When the transaction is complete, the NL_Port closes the temporary connection, making the transport available to others.

4.2.1 Loop Physical Topology

Arbitrated Loop is a true physical loop, or ring, created by tying the transmit lead of one NL_Port to the receive lead of its downstream neighbor. The neighbor's transmit is, in turn, connected to the receiver of yet another NL_Port, and so on, until the circle completes at the original NL_Port's receiver. In this way, a continuous data path exists through all the NL_Ports, allowing any device to access any other device on the loop, as illustrated in Figure 4-2.

The first Arbitrated Loops were built in this fashion, using copper or fiber-optic cabling to create the daisy chain of NL_Ports. Several problems quickly arose. Powering off or disconnecting a single node would break the chain and thus crash the loop. A break in cabling or faulty transceiver anywhere along the loop would also halt loop traffic and entail tedious troubleshooting to locate the problem. Similar to the problems encountered in hardwired Token Ring topologies, the overhead and risks associated with dispersed loop cabling promoted the development of centralized Arbitrated Loop hubs.

Arbitrated Loop hubs provide a physical star topology for a loop configuration, bringing each NL_Port's transmit and receive leads to a common location. The internal architecture of a hub completes the connections between transmitters and receivers on a port-by-port basis via mux (multiplexer) circuitry and finishes the loop by connecting the transmitter of the last hub port (for example, port 12) to the receiver of the first (for example, port 1). One of the most useful features of a hub is bypass circuitry at each port, which allows the loop to circumvent a disabled or disconnected node while maintaining operation. Most unmanaged Arbitrated Loop hubs also validate proper gigabit signaling before allowing a device to insert into the loop, whereas managed hubs provide additional functionality. These features will be described in more detail in Chapter 5.

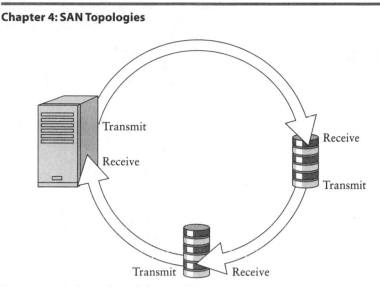

Figure 4-2 *A daisy chain Arbitrated Loop*

Since an Arbitrated Loop hub supplies a limited number of ports, building larger loops may require linking multiple hubs. This is called hub **cascading**. As shown in Figure 4-3, a cascade is simply a normal cable connection between a port on one hub and a port on another. No special cable is required, although to minimize potential ground loop and noise problems, fiber-optic cabling is recommended over copper. Cascading consumes one port on the first and last hubs in a chain and two ports on intervening hubs. Cascading four 6-port hubs, for example, would yield 18 usable ports, with a fourth of the total ports sacrificed to achieve the cascade. Depending on the vendor, hubs can be cascaded to the Arbitrated Loop maximum of 127 ports, although the advisability of doing so should be application-driven. Just because some configurations *can* be built does not mean that they *should* be.

Cascading one hub to another extends the loop through the additional ports on the downstream hub. A similar effect is achieved by inserting a JBOD (just a bunch of disks) into a hub port. Although the link between the hub and the JBOD consists of a single cable pair, the JBOD itself comprises of a series of Arbitrated Loop disks daisy chained (transmit to receive) together. The transmit and receive leads of the JBOD interface to the hub represents not a single NL_Port but an entire cluster, or loop segment, of multiple NL_Ports. The loop is

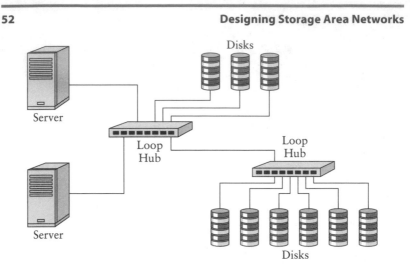

Figure 4-3 *Cascaded Arbitrated Loop hubs*

thus extended through the JBOD enclosure and the loop population increased by the number of drives in the JBOD chassis. This is an important consideration when calculating hub port requirements and optimal loop size.

Arbitrated Loop standards provide address space for up to 127 (126 NL_Ports and 1 FL_Port) devices on one loop. Fibre Channel specifications allow for 10-km runs over single-mode cabling and long-wave fiber-optic transceivers. The reader is advised *not* to combine these two concepts. Even a few 10-km links on a single loop can severely impede loop performance, since each 10-km link incurs a 50-microsecond propagation delay in each direction. Every transaction on the loop would have to traverse the extended links, multiplying the effect of each transit delay by the number of transactions. Long-haul requirements for disaster recovery or campus networks are better served with dedicated switch ports, with attached loops at either end for local traffic.

4.2.2 Loop Addressing

An NL_Port, like an N_Port, has a 24-bit port address. If no switch connection exists, the upper 2 bytes of this port address are zeroed to x′00 00′. This is referred to as **private loop**, since devices on the loop have no connection to the outside world. If the loop is attached to a fabric *and* an NL_Port supports fabric login, the upper 2 bytes (and possibly the last byte) are assigned a positive value by the switch. This mode is called **public loop**, since fabric-capable NL_Ports are members of both a local loop and a greater fabric community and need a full 24-bit address for identity in the network. In the case of public loop assignment, the value of the upper 2 bytes represents the **loop identifier** and would be common to all NL_Ports on the same loop that performed login to the fabric.

In both public and private Arbitrated Loops, the last byte of the 24-bit port address is referred to as the Arbitrated Loop Physical Address, or AL_PA. The AL_PA is acquired during initialization of the loop and may, in the case of fabric-capable loop devices, be modified by the switch during login. The 1-byte AL_PA provides a very compact addressing scheme and allows a device's identity to be included as part of a 4-byte ordered set. In fact, an ordered set may include two AL_PAs, identifying both source and destination devices. The ordered set for Open Full Duplex, for example, is "K28.5 D17.4 AL_PD AL_PS," with AL_PD representing the destination address and AL_PS representing the source address.

The total number of AL_PAs available for Arbitrated Loop addressing is 127. This number was not determined by rigorous performance testing on assorted loop topologies; nor was it calculated on theoretical throughput given various loop populations. It is based instead on the requirements of 8b/10b running disparity between frames. As a frame terminates with an end-of-frame character, the EOF forces the current running disparity negative. By Fibre Channel standard, each transmission word between the end of one frame and the beginning of another should also leave the running disparity negative. This function is provided by the IDLE ordered set, which has a fixed format of K28.5 D21.4 D21.5 D21.5. The special K28.5 leaves running disparity positive. The D21.4 leaves the running disparity negative. The D21.5 characters used for the last 2 bytes are neutral disparity. The net result is a negative running disparity at the end of the IDLE transmission word.

Since the loop-specific ordered sets may include AL_PAs in the last 2 byte positions, negative running disparity is facilitated if these values are neutral. In the Open Full Duplex ordered set cited previously, for example, the D17.4 character following the special K28.5 would leave the running disparity negative. If the destination and source AL_PAs are neutral disparity, the Open transmission word will leave the running disparity negative. This satisfies the requirement for the next start of frame (SOF).

If all 256 possible 8-bit bytes are dispatched to the 8b/10b encoder, 134 will emerge with neutral disparity characters. Fibre Channel claims some of these for special purposes. The remaining 127 neutral disparity characters have been assigned as AL_PAs.

The number "127" is thus not a recommended load for a 100MBps shared transport. It is simply the maximum number (minus reserved values) of neutral disparity addresses that could be assigned for loop use. At higher Fibre Channel speeds, such as 400MBps, 127 active loop participants may be quite reasonable or even considered inadequate for some needs.

Since the AL_PA values are determined on the basis of neutral disparity, a listing of hex values of AL_PAs seems to jump randomly over some byte values and not others. Listed sequentially, the hex value of AL_PAs would begin 00, 01, 02, 04, 08, 0F, 10, 17, 18, 1B, 1D, ... The gaps in the list represent byte values that, after 8b/10b encoding, result in nonneutral disparity characters. This is significant for some Fibre Channel disk drives, which allow the user to set jumpers or dip switches on a controller card to assign a fixed AL_PA manually. Typically, the jumper positions correspond only to an index of AL_PA values, not to actual hex values, which is the case with most network equipment.

Arbitrated Loop assigns priority to AL_PAs, based on numeric value. The lower the numeric value, the higher the priority. AL_PA priority is used during arbitration to give advantage to initiators, such as file servers and fabric loop ports. An FL_Port by default has the address x'00', which gives it the highest priority over all other NL_Ports. When arbitrating against other devices for access to the loop, the FL_Port will always win. This helps ensure that a valuable resource, such as a switch, can quickly service the loop and then return to fabric duties. During address selection, as shown in Figure 4-4, servers typically attempt to take the highest-priority, lowest-value AL_PAs, whereas disk arrays take lower-priority, higher-value AL_PAs. A server with an AL_PA of x'01' will have a statistically higher chance of winning arbitration against lower-priority contenders,

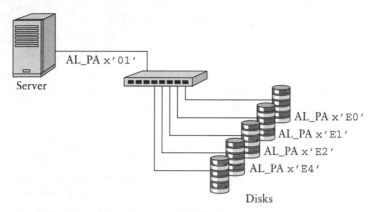

Figure 4-4 *AL_PA assignment on a small loop*

although Arbitrated Loop also provides safeguards against starvation of any port.

An NL_Port's AL_PA may change with every initialization of the loop or reset of the device. On the surface, this may seem disruptive, but dynamic address assignment by the topology itself greatly reduces administrative overhead. As anyone who has had to reconfigure an IP network can testify, offloading low-level address administration to the topology is highly desirable. Arbitrated Loop initialization guarantees that each attached device will have a unique AL_PA. Potential addressing conflicts are possible only when two separate loops are joined together—for example, by cascading two active hubs—without initialization. Some hub vendors have responded to this problem by incorporating an initialization sequence whenever a cascade condition is sensed.

4.2.3 Loop Initialization

Loop initialization is an essential process for allowing new participants onto the loop, assigning AL_PAs, providing notification of topology changes, and recovering from loop failure. Following loop initialization, the loop enters a stable monitoring mode and begins (or resumes) normal activity. Depending on the number of NL_Ports attached to the loop, an entire loop initialization sequence may take only a few milliseconds. For Sun Solaris servers, a loop initialization may result in a message posted to the event log. For NT servers, it is largely ignored. In either case, a loop initialization on an active loop normally causes a brief suspension of activity, which resumes once initialization is complete.

A loop initialization may be triggered by a number of causes, the most common being the introduction of a new device. The new device could be a former participant that has been powered on or an active device that has been moved from one hub port to another.

A number of ordered sets has been defined to cover the various conditions that an NL_Port may sense as it launches the initialization process. These ordered sets are Loop Initialization Primitive sequences and are referred to collectively as **LIPs**. An NL_Port issues at least 12 LIPs to start loop initialization. In the following examples, we will assume a Fibre Channel host bus adapter installed in a file server.

- An HBA that is attached to an active loop and is power cycled will, on bootup, start processing the incoming bit stream. The presence of valid signal and protocol verifies that the server is on an active loop. Because the server was powered down, however, the HBA has lost the AL_PA that it was previously assigned. That previously assigned AL_PA was stored in a temporary register in the HBA, and the register was wiped clean by the power cycle. The HBA immediately begins transmitting **LIP(F7, F7)** onto the loop. The xF7 is a reserved, neutral disparity character. The first occurrence of xF7 indicates that the HBA recognizes that it is on an active loop. The second xF7 indicates that the HBA has no AL_PA.

- An HBA that is attached to an active loop is moved from one hub port to another. As the cable is unplugged from the hub and moved to the other port, the HBA temporarily loses Fibre Channel signal. On reinsertion, the HBA sees valid signal return and begins processing the bit stream. In this instance, the HBA still has its previously assigned AL_PA and so begins transmitting **LIP(F7, AL_PS)** onto the loop. The xF7 indicates that the HBA sees the active loop. The AL_PS is the source AL_PA of the LIP, that is, the HBA's previously assigned AL_PA. In this example, the HBA is not issuing LIPs in order to acquire an address but to notify the loop that a topology change has occurred.

- The receiver of the HBA or the receive cable is broken, and the server has been power cycled. In this instance, the HBA does not see a valid signal on its receiver and assumes that a loop failure has occurred. It also does not recall its previously assigned AL_PA. The HBA therefore starts streaming **LIP(F8, F7)** onto the loop. The xF8 is another reserved, neutral disparity character that is used to indicate a loop-down state. The xF7 indicates that the HBA has no AL_PA.

- In the same scenario, if the HBA still has a previously assigned AL_PA, it will issue a **LIP(F8, AL_PS)**. The xF8 indicates that the HBA senses loop failure. The AL_PS is the source AL_PA of the alert.

Of the conditions listed, the most insidious for Arbitrated Loop environments is the LIP(F8) stream. A node issuing a normal LIP(F7) will trigger, at most, a temporary suspension of loop operations until the initialization process is completed. A node issuing LIP(F8)s, however, will continue streaming loop-down alarms as long as it cannot recognize loop activity on its receiver. If the node's transmitter is connected to an active loop, all NL_Ports will enter a suspended initialization state and continue to forward the offender's LIP(F8) stream, as shown in Figure 4-5. Normal loop initialization cannot complete, and the loop in fact fails. This has been another challenge for Arbitrated Loop hub vendors. Some have responded with autorecovery policies that automatically bypass a port that is streaming LIP(F8)s.

In addition to loss of signal, an NL_Port may LIP(F8) if no valid ordered sets are present on the loop. This may occur if an upstream node is corrupting the bit stream, due to excessive jitter or malfunction of processing logic. Other conditions may trigger LIPs, including a node's inability to arbitrate successfully for loop access. Arbitrated Loop provides a fairness algorithm for media access, but if a participant is not playing fairly, others on the loop may LIP to reinitialize a level playing field. Arbitrated Loop also provides a selective reset LIP that is directed by one NL_Port to another. How the reset is implemented is vendor-specific, but the selective reset LIP(AL_PD, AL_PS)

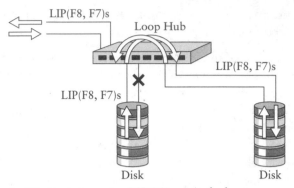

Figure 4-5 *An NL_Port streaming LIP(F8)s onto the loop*

may cause the target device to reboot. This allows one NL_Port to force a misbehaving NL_Port into a known good state.

The loop initialization process begins when an NL_Port streams at least 12 LIPs onto the loop. As each downstream device receives the LIP stream, the device enters a state known as Open-Init, which suspends any current operations and prepares the device for the loop initialization procedure. The LIPs are forwarded along the loop until all NL_Ports, including the originator, are in an Open-Init condition.

At this point, the NL_Ports need someone to be in charge. Unlike Token Ring, Arbitrated Loop has no permanent master to monitor the topology. Loop initialization therefore provides a selection process to determine which device will be the temporary loop master. Once selected, the loop master is responsible for conducting the rest of the initialization procedure and returning the loop to normal operation. See Figure 4-6.

The loop master is determined by a subroutine known as the Loop Initialization Select Master procedure, or LISM. Each loop device vies for the position of temporary master by continuously issuing LISM frames, which contain a port type identifier (x'00' for FL_Port, x'EF' for NL_Port) and its 64-bit World-Wide Name. As a downstream device receives a LISM frame from an upstream partner, the device first checks the identifier. If the identifier is x'00', a fabric is present, and the device ceases is own LISM frame broadcast and begins issuing the FL_Port's LISM frame. If the identifier is a standard NL_Port, the downstream device compares the World-Wide Name in the LISM

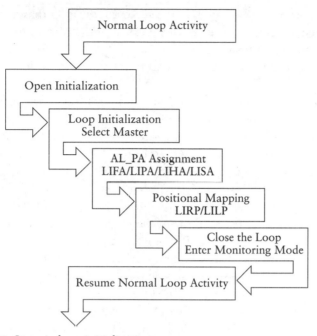

Figure 4-6 *Steps in loop initialization sequence*

frame to its own. As with AL_PA priorities, the World-Wide Name with the lowest numeric value has highest priority. If the received World-Wide Name has higher priority, the device ceases its own LISM broadcast and begins transmitting the received LISM. If the received World-Wide Name has lower priority, the device throws the received LISM away and continues broadcasting its own LISM. Eventually, a node will receive its own LISM frame, indicating that it has the highest priority and is therefore temporary loop master. The node then begins transmitting a special ordered set, ARB(F0), to notify the others that a temporary master has been selected; as the ARB(F0) circles back to the loop master, the initialization can proceed to the next phase.

The first task of the temporary loop master is to issue a series of four frames that will allow each participant on the loop to select a unique AL_PA. The frame format contains a 128-bit field that represents an abbreviated mapping of all possible AL_PAs. The position of each bit in the AL_PA map corresponds to the sequential list of AL_PAs, beginning with x'00' and ending with x'EF'. When the first frame is issued, all bits are initialized to 0, indicating that no AL_PAs have been selected. As each device picks an AL_PA from the map, the corresponding bit is set to 1.

The header of each AL_PA map frame contains an identifier that defines which loop device is allowed to select an AL_PA. The first frame issued has an identifier of Loop Initialization Fabric Address, or LIFA. As this frame circulates the loop, only public loop devices that had previously been assigned an address by the fabric have permission to select a bit corresponding to their original AL_PA. When this frame returns to the loop master, the frame is reissued with a Loop Initialization Previous Address, or LIPA, identifier. Now, the private loop devices that remember their previously assigned AL_PAs have an opportunity to reselect them from the map. If by chance two devices previously had the same AL_PA—for example, if two separate, active loops were hot cascaded—the first device to see the frame would be able to reselect it. The second device would see the bit already set to 1 and would have to wait for the next frame.

As the frame is issued for the third time, the identifier is changed to Loop Initialization Hard Address, or LIHA. NL_Ports that have dip switch or jumpered addresses, such as disk drive controllers, may now attempt to select AL_PAs from the map corresponding to their hard-wired addresses. If the hard-assigned AL_PA is already taken, however, a device must wait for the next addressing frame. The last frame issued has an identifier of Loop Initialization Soft Address, or LISA. This frame is for any NL_Ports that did not qualify for or were unsuccessful in the previous rounds. On a populous, previously operational loop, devices that must select from the LISA frame would find only leftovers. Typically, an initiator, such as a server, will attempt to select a bit corresponding to a higher-priority AL_PA; a target, such as a disk, may attempt to select a lower-priority AL_PA.

Once the LISA frame returns to the temporary loop master, each loop device will have a unique AL_PA. In the original Fibre Channel standard for Arbitrated Loop (FC-AL-1), the loop initialization process was closed after this phase, and the loop returned to normal operation. As an option, vendors could implement an additional sub-routine to provide positional mapping of devices along the loop. A positional map is useful for determining how AL_PAs are physically positioned in a loop topology. Knowing which AL_PAs are on which hub ports, for example, provides diagnostic capability and opportunity to fine-tune a loop configuration for optimal performance.

One problem with the positional mapping subroutine, however, is that not all Arbitrated Loop devices support it. The HP Tachyon chip set, for example, is widely used in host bus adapters and disk controllers and was designed before positional mapping was developed. FC-AL-2 accommodates these devices by providing LISA frame header bits that can be set by Tachyon or other nonparticipants. If any device reports that it cannot support positional mapping, the subroutine is abandoned, and the temporary loop master closes the initialization process. Otherwise, the loop master issues a Loop Initialization Report Position, or LIRP, frame, which may contain up to 127 bytes. The temporary loop master inserts its own AL_PA in the first byte position, increments an offset by 1, and passes the frame downstream. As each loop device receives the LIRP, it inserts its AL_PA in the next byte position, increments the offset, and forwards the frame. Eventually, the frame fills with a positional map that details how loop devices are physically positioned in relationship to one another. When the positional map is complete, the loop master distributes it in a Loop Initialization Loop Position, or LILP, frame, allowing each loop device to copy and process the contents.

As long as the positional map is used for diagnostic or optimization purposes, the failure of Tachyon or other Fibre Channel controllers to support it does not create interoperability problems. Some vendors, however, use the positional map to discover what devices are on the loop. Instead of polling through the entire 127 AL_PA address space to discover targets, these implementations poll only those AL_PAs listed in the positional map. Consequently, interoperability may be an issue when mixing Tachyon and positional map-dependent devices on the same loop.

Following the LILP—if all devices support positional mapping—or LISA—if some do not—the temporary master finishes loop initialization by issuing a Close (CLS) ordered set, followed by IDLEs. As each loop device receives the CLS, it leaves the Open-Init state and resumes normal operation. IDLEs continue to circulate around the loop until any previously suspended operations are resumed or new ones begun.

It is helpful to remember that although this discussion of the initialization process is somewhat lengthy, the process completes in mere milliseconds and is generally nondisruptive to loop operations.

The variables introduced by loop initialization are important considerations for SAN design. In any network, failures occur most frequently during adds, moves, and changes. Proper selection of components, HBAs, disks, and Arbitrated Loop hubs will help ensure that the topology change that loop initialization implies will not impact loop stability.

4.2.4 Port Login

Loop initialization allows each device to select a unique AL_PA and thus avoids addressing conflict on the loop. A loop with a single server and 24 Fibre Channel disk drives will emerge from loop initialization with 25 distinct AL_PAs. Immediately following loop initialization, however, the server has no idea what else is on the loop. For an initiator (server) to discover targets (disks), an additional step is required. This function is provided by a port-to-port login process known as **N_Port login**, or **PLOGI**. A similar function, known as **Fabric Login** (**FLOGI**), is provided for fabric-capable devices. Both login processes are part of a set of Extended Link Services, which are used to exchange communication parameters and identities and thus to establish logical sessions between devices on the topology.

In Arbitrated Loop, PLOGI is usually performed immediately following loop initialization. Since Fibre Channel disk drives do not normally communicate with one another—except in XOR drive configurations—there is no need for a disk to initiate a device discovery. A server, on the other hand, will need to discover all targets on the loop, even if the upper-layer application, such as NT Disk Administrator, assigns only a few for the server's use. In most implementations, the server attempts to establish login sessions with targets by issuing PLOGI frames addressed to each of the 126 possible NL_Port AL_PAs. The targets that accept the PLOGI from the server will return an ACC (Accept) frame to the server, informing it of the target's World-Wide Name, buffer-to-buffer credit capability, maximum frame size support, and so on. By thus walking the address space, the server finds and establishes sessions with active participants on the loop.

The PLOGI login session is the first step in a series of exchanges between loop devices, percolating up through the Fibre Channel hierarchy to FC-4's upper-protocol-layer interface. At some point, an association must be made between the link-level AL_PAs and the application's logical definition of SCSI bus, target, and LUN (logical unit number) addressing. The Extended Link Services that interface to FC-2 can determine what is out there; FC-4, such as Fiber Channel Protocol for SCSI-3, can then determine what can be done with them. The responsibility for maintaining the association between lower-level AL_PAs and upper-level SCSI addressing is assumed by the device driver of the HBA or controller installed in an initiator.

4.2.5 Loop Port State Machine

Arbitrated Loop introduces to Fibre Channel architecture a new functional layer that resides between the FC-1 encoding/decoding function and FC-2's frame management and flow control functions. Loop-specific functions are embodied in the Loop Port State Machine, and the state machine, in turn, is embedded in silicon or microcode in Fibre Channel loop end nodes. See Figure 4-7.

The Loop Port State Machine is responsible for monitoring and performing the actions required to become a loop participant, accessing the loop for transactions, being opened for transactions by other devices, and yielding control of the loop when transactions are complete. These processes are expressed in 11 states and are controlled by

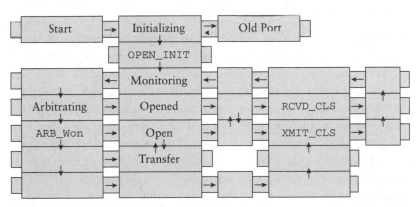

Figure 4-7 *Loop Port State Machine Logic*

a number of input and output variables. As requests are handed down by the FC-2 layer, the Loop Port State Machine must determine its current state and what further actions are required to fulfill the pending request. If, for example, the upper layer has frames to send, the Loop Port State Machine must transition from its normal monitoring state and enter an arbitrating state to gain access to the loop. When it wins arbitration, the Loop Port State Machine changes to an ARB_Won state, and then to an open state as it notifies the target that a transaction is under way. When the frame transmission is complete, the Loop Port State Machine will enter a transmitted close (XMIT_CLS) or received close (RCVD_CLS) state and finally return to monitoring mode.

Depending on its current state, the Loop Port State Machine may not be able to service upper-layer requests immediately. FC-2 could have frames pending, but the Loop Port State Machine may already be in an opened state; that is, another loop device has it conditioned to receive frames. Or, the Loop Port State Machine may be in an open state and in the midst of frame transfer when a LIP is received, in which case the Loop Port State Machine must suspend any current activity and enter the Open-Init state. The logical transition from one state to another, based on current inputs and variables, provides an efficient mechanism for orderly conduct of the loop. Early interoperability testing of vendors' implementations of Loop Port State Machine logic revealed a number of timing and transition issues, but current interoperability is quite high.

4.2.6 Arbitration

Since Arbitrated Loop is a shared transport, gaining access to the loop is a central function of the Loop Port State Machine. Contention for access involves two components: the priority of a loop device's AL_PA and an access variable that is toggled when a device wins arbitration. An NL_Port that observes fairness in sharing the loop will, after it has won arbitration, reset its access bit and be able to arbitrate again only when no other devices are arbitrating. This scheme allows even low-priority devices on the loop to win arbitration and thus prevents starvation of any port. Fabric loop ports, however, do not play fairly. If an FL_Port honored fair access, the switch might become congested as frames queued up at the FL_Port for delivery to the loop. Because an

FL_Port is unfair and has the highest-priority AL_PA, it is always assured of winning arbitration whenever it needs loop access.

An arbitrate primitive, ARB(x), is transmitted whenever a loop device needs access to the loop. The format of the primitive is "K28.5 D20.4 AL_PA AL_PA" but is referred to generically as ARB(x) to indicate that each of the last 2 bytes contains the AL_PA of the arbitrating device. An ARB(x) may be transmitted even if another NL_Port owns the loop, but if frames are traversing the loop, the ARB(x) can be issued only between frames. The ARB(x) is transmitted by substituting an ARB for each current fill word (CFW). When no frame traffic is on the loop, the current fill word is normally the IDLE primitive. Passing through the arbitrating NL_Port, each IDLE is replaced with an ARB(x) containing the AL_PA of the arbitrator. If another device already possesses the loop, the current fill word will be ARB(F0). The x'F0' in this primitive has the lowest priority and is used as an indicator for the fairness algorithm. As we will see, the arbitrating device will substitute its own ARB(x) for the ARB(F0) received.

If no other device is arbitrating, the NL_Port will transmit an ARB(x) with its own AL_PA value and, as the ARB(x) circles the loop, it will be returned to the sender. The NL_Port would then transition to the ARB_Won state and proceed to an OPEN condition to send frames. If two or more devices are arbitrating at the same time, the NL_Port with the highest-priority AL_PA will win. As an arbitrating device receives an ARB(x) from an upstream partner, the device compares the value of the AL_PA to its own. If the received ARB(x) carries a higher-priority AL_PA, the device must forward it on. If the received ARB(x) contains a lower-priority AL_PA, the device replaces the received ARB(x) with its own. In this way, only the NL_Port with the highest-priority AL_PA will receive its own ARB(x) and thus win arbitration. The contending arbitrators will continue issuing their own ARB(x)s and will continue to substitute their ARB(x) for any received lower-priority ARB(x) until they too eventually win arbitration.

Fairness is monitored by the presence of the ARB(F0) primitive on the loop. When a loop device wins arbitration, it sets its access variable to 0. As long as the access bit is 0, the device cannot arbitrate again. The winning device also begins substituting all current fill words it receives with ARB(F0). These ARB(F0) primitives are forwarded by nonarbitrating devices around the loop. If another NL_Port begins arbitrating, it will compare the AL_PA value in any received ARB(F0) to its own. The xF0 will always have lowest priority, and consequently the contending NL_Port will substitute its own ARB(x) for the stream of ARB(F0)s it receives. When the contender's ARB(x) is received by the current arbitration winner, the contender informs the current loop owner that another device is still arbitrating. The current loop owner discards the received ARB(x) and again substitutes ARB(F0).

When it is finished with the loop, the current owner yields control of the loop to others. Its access variable, however, is still set to 0 and cannot be reset as long as ARB(F0)s are circulating. The next-highest-priority AL_PA that is arbitrating will immediately win and begin the same process of ARB(F0) substitution. As long as active arbitrators are contending for loop access, ARB(F0)s will continue to stream from the current winner, and this, in turn, will keep the access bits of all previous winners set to 0. The duration of this activity is called the **access fairness window**. The window is closed only when a current winner receives an ARB(F0). The fact that no other loop device substituted an ARB(x) for the ARB(F0) in transit back to the current winner confirms that no other devices are arbitrating. When the current winner closes its transaction and yields control of the loop, it ceases issuing ARB(F0)s and replaces the current fill word with IDLEs. As each previous winner receives IDLEs, its access bit is reset to 1, and it is now free to arbitrate at will.

The arbitration strategy has design implications for SANs, since it may be helpful to manipulate fairness to increase performance. Allowing certain file servers to be unfair will increase their access to disks in terms of less critical servers.

4.2.7 Nonbroadcast Nature of Arbitrated Loop

Shared LAN topologies, such as Ethernet and Token Ring, are broadcast transports, in that data sent by any device on a segment is broadcast to all other devices on the same segment. Ethernet is an obvious example, since an Ethernet transmission is sent along a common wire for all to hear. Each device along the wire processes the transmission to determine whether the destination MAC address matches its own. Token Ring uses a similar transmit-to-receive cabling scheme as Arbitrated Loop. A Token Ring device waits for a free token to pass by, marks the token busy and appends its data, and forwards the frame downstream. As it receives the frame, each Token Ring device examines the destination MAC address for a match. If the frame is addressed to the device, it marks the frame copied and forwards it on to the ring. Eventually, the original frame returns to the sender. The sender sees that the frame was copied, removes the frame from the ring, and issues a new free token.

Because transmissions are visible to any device on an Ethernet or Token Ring segment, capturing traffic for problem diagnosis is relatively straightforward. A Network Associates Sniffer can be plugged into any hub port for data capture of all segment activity. Multiple conversations between multiple pairs of devices can be captured on a single trace without moving the Sniffer from port to port. Once the capture is complete, decoding of frames and analysis of protocol or performance problems can proceed.

Arbitrated Loop, unlike Ethernet or Token Ring, is a nonbroadcast transport. When an NL_Port wins arbitration and opens a target for frame transmission, a frame or series of frames may be sent from initiator to target. Intervening loop devices in the path between the two will see the frames and forward them. The target, or recipient, however, removes the frames from the loop and simply issues an R_RDY or CLS primitive to the sender. The loop devices downstream from the recipient will forward the primitive back to the initiator but have no visibility to the frame transaction that occurred. See Figure 4-8. During normal loop operation, the nonbroadcast nature of Arbitrated Loop enhances performance by removing frame-handling overhead from at least part of the loop.

Because frames are not broadcast throughout the loop segment, capturing traffic for problem diagnosis in Arbitrated Loops is more challenging. With most Fibre Channel analyzers, it is possible to capture only traffic going into and out of a single port. Instead of simply plugging into any available hub port, analyzer probes must be placed in ports immediately preceding and following the monitored port or must be configured inline on the monitored device's link. This requirement alone is disruptive to loop traffic and may, in fact, mask an intermittent problem by altering the topology. Some Arbitrated Loop hub vendors have responded to these difficulties by engineering analyzer functionality into the hub.

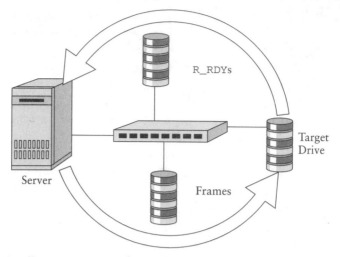

R_RDYs

Target
Drive

Server   Frames

Figure 4-8 *Frame transit in Arbitrated Loop*

4.2.8 Design Considerations for Arbitrated Loop

The first question that should be asked when designing any network topology is, *What's the application?* The application requirements for prepress operations, for example, which require only intermittent transfers of very large graphics files, are different from those for sustained full-motion video. Requirements for casual database queries for customer information systems are different from those for tape-backup applications. High-availability networks require redundancy of data and data paths, whereas less mission-critical applications do not.

Unfortunately, many enterprise and information networks have evolved in a reactionary mode to the introduction of new applications. Only when a new application is deployed by one department is it discovered that the existing network infrastructure cannot accommodate the bandwidth or connectivity requirements. As a consequence, some networks are constructed with an eclectic array of routers, switches, and gateways that were selected in a crisis atmosphere to address quickly problems that could have been foreseen.

Because SANs are a completely new, scalable network topology, they offer an opportunity to size the network rationally to application needs. The mere decision to deploy a SAN indicates that one level of application analysis has been performed. The decision to institute

LAN-free tape backup across a SAN, for example, reveals the determination that the LAN transport is incapable of supporting the bandwidth and backup window required and that a separate network is needed for storage.

Arbitrated Loops are not suited to every application requirement, but they do provide an economical solution for a wide variety of data needs. Among the application-driven criteria that should be considered when implementing Arbitrated Loops are

- Types of devices per loop segment
- Private and public loop support
- Total number of loop devices per segment
- Bandwidth requirements
- Distance requirements
- Managed or unmanaged environments
- High availability requirements

Additional issues also factor into the design equation, especially since SANs are often required to support multiple, sometimes contending, applications concurrently. Balancing the needs of each application on a common topology may be challenging, which is why complex SANs are often constructed with a combination of shared-loop segments and fabrics.

Types of Devices per Loop Segment: An Arbitrated Loop may support a variety of devices, including host bus adapters installed in servers, individual Fibre Channel disk drives, JBODs, Fibre Channel RAIDs (redundant arrays of independent disks), native Fibre Channel tape subsystems, and Fibre Channel–to–SCSI bridges. At the link level, each device type simply appears as one or more AL_PAs or as peers on a common transport. At the upper-layer protocol, the device types divide into a less egalitarian society of initiators and targets.

Since applications sit on top of the upper-layer protocol of initiators, they typically determine the traffic patterns to and from targets. Read-intensive applications, such as data mining, create a traffic flow from target to initiator. Tape-backup applications create a flow from initiator to target or, in the case of Third Party Copy backup, from target to a hybrid target. For single-initiator loops, mixing multiple device types on the same topology has little impact, since the initiator is responsible for launching all transactions, such as reads and writes to disk or tape. The physical positioning of devices on the loop can therefore be optimized for the dominant application of that initiator. In multi-initiator environments, optimization via physical positioning of devices is more difficult.

Tape backup presents a special problem for multi-initiator loops. Tape subsystems connected through Fibre Channel–to–SCSI bridges or native Fibre Channel interface are not particularly fast—typically less than 15MBps—and so pose no bandwidth issues. A streaming tape backup, however, cannot tolerate interruption. A disruption to the backup data stream may abort the entire process, defeating tape's prime directive of data security. In the more dynamic and populous loop environment, which a multi-initiator configuration implies, the statistical occurrence of interruptions in the form of LIPs increases. Installing a new drive in a JBOD while a tape is backing up another array, for example, will initiate a LIP throughout the loop segment and will, potentially, abort the backup process. Segregating tape-backup systems to fabric ports or restricting LIP propagation via intelligent hubs is therefore strongly recommended, provided that the AL_PAs are managed via hard addressing.

If multiple initiators and multiple targets share the same loop, can all servers access the same drives? The topology guarantees that they can but will not guarantee the consequences if they do. Arbitrated Loop does not provide intrinsic file locking, file permission monitoring, volume ownership, or any other feature that would prevent two servers from overwriting data on the same drive. If required, data sharing among multiple initiators can be accomplished with middleware, usually in the form of applications that sit between the operating system and SCSI-3. Otherwise, manual administration is required to ensure that each target is owned by a single initiator.

This problem is aggravated by Windows NT, since NT wants to own everything it sees. When an NT server boots on an Arbitrated Loop (or fabric), NT Disk Administrator will query and report all Fibre Channel–attached drives. If the drive has not previously been accessed or formatted for NT, Disk Administrator will immediately prompt the user to write a volume label on the disk so that it can be accessed. If the user consents, a volume label will be written to the first sector of the disk, which, if the disk belongs to a Solaris server, will make the disk and its files unusable. Although the number of initiators on the same segment is important in terms of administering disk ownership, heterogeneous operating systems and their appetites should also be considered. Fibre Channel fabrics and switching hubs with port zoning (discussed below) are possible solutions for mixed OS (operating system) environments.

Private and Public Loop Support: Most departmental application requirements are readily satisfied by the bandwidth and population restrictions of private Arbitrated Loop. With one to four servers and several RAID or JBOD arrays, a customer service, engineering, or similar department would have adequate storage and response time for data access. The vast majority of installed Fibre Channel configurations in use are based on departmental, private Arbitrated Loops.

Support for fabric login and public loop becomes meaningful when bandwidth allocation, population, or distance requirements exceed the capabilities of a single loop. Introducing a fabric opens new design possibilities for loop configurations but also mandates fabric support for HBAs, disks, and other loop devices. With a large installed base of nonfabric, private loop devices in the market, some switch vendors have engineered support for both public and private loop devices on the same fabric.

For new SAN installations, it is preferable to select components that support public loop, even if the initial configuration is a standalone Arbitrated Loop. This is not a consideration for selecting Arbitrated Loop hubs, since they play a passive role in the loop and have no login functions. Selecting host bus adapters and storage devices with fabric login capability, however, will provide additional flexibility in evolving the SAN and will extend the life of the investment.

Total Number of Loop Devices per Segment: As discussed previously, the capacity of a single Arbitrated Loop—126 NL_Ports and 1 FL_Port—was not derived from performance calculations but is the result of neutral disparity requirements. What is a reasonable maximum number of devices that can be configured on a single loop? It depends on the application. Theoretically, a SAN design could specify a lone file server and 125 disks on a single Arbitrated Loop. Some vendor implementations, in fact, have a single server with more than 90

Fibre Channel drives on a single loop. These large loop configurations are not unreasonable when only one or two files servers are present and are not aggressively contending for bandwidth. The obvious benefit of such large loops is storage capacity. Over a terabyte of storage can be provided by 125 10GB Fibre Channel drives.

Arbitrated Loops, especially ones with multiple initiators, normally do not exceed 20–30 devices. Most are much smaller, in the 2–10 device range, depending on whether Fibre Channel RAIDs or JBODs are used for storage. Host bus adapters are capable of driving over 97MBps, or nearly the full Fibre Channel bandwidth. Fibre Channel drives may provide 15MBps–18MBps throughput each. If a server uses software RAID to stripe data blocks across multiple drives, a JBOD of eight drives can fulfill server requests at nearly the same throughput as the HBA. From a performance standpoint, adding more JBODs to this nine-node loop will not significantly affect total throughput but will simply make additional storage available. Additional initiators, however, may degrade performance if the new servers are equally contending for access *and* the application has high bandwidth requirements, such as video.

Bandwidth Requirements: In the preceding example, a configuration with one server, equipped with an efficient HBA, and an eight-drive JBOD provided enough throughput nearly to saturate a 100MBps Fibre Channel pipe. For the pipe to be utilized fully, the application would have to drive a sustained access to disk. In reality, this occurs only with specialized applications, such as multiple streams of full-motion video. At 100MBps, Arbitrated Loop is capable of supporting several video streams, primarily because such streams use the maximum 2,112-byte frame payload and require less command overhead per transaction.

Most enterprise applications do not require sustained throughput. Radiology, geological resource mapping, prepress, and other applications that require very large file transfers, for example, tend to be bursty, with periods of extremely high utilization followed by periods of inactivity. Determining the total bandwidth requirements of such applications is difficult, since averaging the total data requirement over time does not address the bandwidth needs of random bursts of data. Other applications, such as online transaction processing (OLTP),

Internet service provider (ISP) Web servers, and relational database queries, may have more predictable bandwidth requirements.

Distance Requirements: Arbitrated Loop is a closed-ring topology, the total circumference being determined by the distances between nodes. At gigabit speeds, signals propagate through copper media at 4 nanoseconds per meter and through fiber-optic media at 5 nanoseconds per meter. The total propagation delay incurred by the loop's circumference can be easily calculated by multiplying the lengths—both transmit and receive—of copper and fiber-optic cabling deployed by the appropriate delay factor. A single 10-kilometer link to an NL_Port, for example, would cause a 50-microsecond propagation delay in each direction, or 100 microseconds total. This is the equivalent of 1MBps of bandwidth consumed to accommodate the link. In practice, the propagation-delay penalty is negligible compared to the degradation long links incur at the protocol level. Since all transactions must traverse a larger circumference, performance may decline by up to 40 percent.

Some applications, such as disaster recovery (Figure 4-9) and campus storage networks, may, depending on bandwidth requirements of locally attached devices, use a single Arbitrated Loop for a few long-distance links. Multiple long runs, however, should be segregated onto fabric ports. This increases the efficiency of the local users and prevents every loop circuit from having to transit an extended topology.

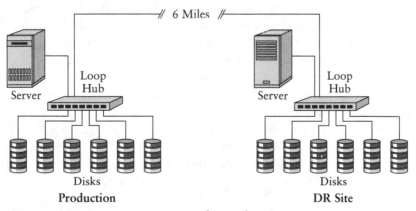

Figure 4-9 *Disaster recovery, using Arbitrated Loop*

Managed or Unmanaged Environments: Advances in Arbitrated Loop hub design have produced products with various levels of management capability, from simple enclosure services to enhanced analyzer-type functionality. Managed hubs usually provide a graphical interface written in Java or platform-specific programming languages. In addition to port density and port cost, the management features available in various products should be considered when selecting loop hubs.

Not all loop environments require management. Applications that are less critical to business operations, loops that support only a few devices, homogeneous (single-vendor) configurations, and so on, may function quite well without management. Mission-critical applications, populous loops, and heterogeneous (multivendor) configurations, however, almost demand the higher level of visibility that management provides. Fibre Channel hardware components, like current networking products in general, are very stable and have a high mean time between failure (MTBF). Even then, a cable will eventually be pulled inadvertently or a host bus adapter will misbehave. When something does break, products with good management features can help reduce down time and restore the loop to operation.

High-Availability Requirements: The traditional SCSI architecture, with its parallel cabling, does not lend itself to high-availability configurations. The networking characteristics of SANs make design and implementation of high availability to storage a much easier task. A common configuration for Arbitrated Loop involves dual-provisioning HBAs in each server and installing two Arbitrated Loop hubs for redundant paths, as shown in Figure 4-10. Fibre Channel disk drives typically provide A and B channels for dual-loop attachment. This configuration provides redundant data paths, as well as redundant loop hubs, transceivers, cables, and power supplies. A failure of one loop will, with the appropriate software running on the host, automatically route data to the standby loop.

High-availability configurations using dual loops are given additional reliability if managed hubs are used for each loop. Knowing the status of both loops—for example, that the standby loop itself has not failed—provides a much higher level of stable operation.

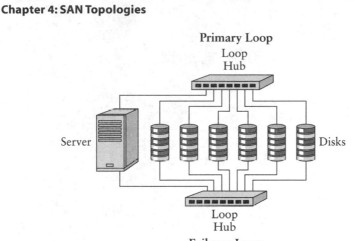

Figure 4-10 *Redundant-loop configuration*

4.3 Fabrics

A Fibre Channel fabric is one or more fabric switches in a single, sometimes extended, configuration. Fabrics provide full 100MBps bandwidth per port. Whereas the introduction of new devices to an Arbitrated Loop further divides the shared bandwidth, adding new devices on each port of a fabric *increases* the aggregate bandwidth. An 8-port fabric with four initiators and four targets, for example, can support four concurrent 100MBps conversations, or a total of 400MBps throughput (800MBps if full-duplex applications were available). See Figure 4-11.

The switching mechanism typically used in fabrics is called **cut-through**. Cut-through technology is also used in Ethernet switches to speed packet routing from port to port. When a frame enters a fabric port from an attached N_Port, cut-through logic examines only the link-level destination ID (D_ID) of the frame. In Fibre Channel, the destination ID is the 24-bit port address of the target N_Port. A routing decision is based on the D_ID, and the frame is switched by internal routing logic to the appropriate port. Cut-through increases performance by reducing the time required to make a routing decision. Since the D_ID resides in the first 4-byte word of the frame header, a

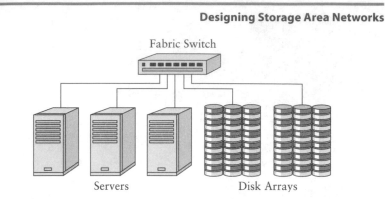

Figure 4-11 *An 8-port fabric*

routing decision can be made immediately as the frame enters the fabric port. Alternatively, the **store-and-forward** algorithm used by some switch technologies requires buffering the entire frame before a routing decision occurs.

The number of frame buffers offered on each F_Port is an important consideration for switch selection. During periods of congestion, the fabric may not be able simply to transmit a frame on the destination port, especially if two N_Ports are sending data to the same destination. Depending on the class of service, the fabric may be forced to abandon frames it cannot process. The ability to queue multiple frames reduces this possibility and enhances performance for both transmitting and receiving N_Ports.

Fabrics, unlike Arbitrated Loop, are not restricted to an address space based on transmission word running disparity (that is, AL_PAs). Fabric-attached N_Ports are assigned a 24-bit port address, which theoretically allows for 2^{24}: more than 16 million possible addresses. The address allocation scheme introduced by the Fibre Channel switch fabric (FC-SW) standard reduces this number somewhat to around 15½ million. Since fabric products available in the market provide 8 to 32 ports, this reduction from 16 to 15½ million addresses has not yet caused an uproar among end users.

The FC-SW standard divides the 3-byte port address into three 1-byte fields: the **Domain**, the most significant; the **Area**, the next most significant; and the **Port**, the least significant. The 8-bit domain field has a number of reserved addresses, leaving 239 available for assignment to individual switches. This allows each switch in an extended

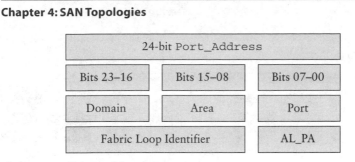

Figure 4-12 *Fabric addressing*

fabric to have a unique identifier and also limits the largest possible fabric to 239 interconnected switches. The 8-bit area field provides 256 area addresses, which can be used to identify individual FL_Ports supporting loops, or groups of F_Ports, such as a multiport blade installed in a switch chassis, that may be governed by a separate part of the routing engine. Finally, the 8-bit port field provides 256 addresses for identifying attached N_Ports or NL_Ports. See Figure 4-12.

The division of the 24 bit address space into domain, area, and port provides enhanced switching performance by enabling a routing decision to be made on the basis of a single byte. If an incoming frame, for example, has a domain address intended for a different switch in the fabric, the routing engine can forward the frame to the appropriate interconnect, or E_Port, without processing the entire 24-bit address.

Fibre Channel switch products offer from 8 ports for departmental fabrics to 64 ports for larger enterprise-level fabrics. Since fabrics are extended via switch-to-switch links on E_Ports, a potential bottleneck could occur during periods of high activity between switches. This problem could be resolved by providing multiple E_Ports between two interconnected switches and a load-balancing algorithm to distribute traffic. Such a solution, however, might result in out-of-order delivery of frames from source to destination, since a sequence of frames could take different paths through the fabric. Consequently, some implementations allow for only a single active link between two switches. If a backup E_Port link is provided, it can be enabled only if the primary E_Port fails. As 2Gbps or 4Gbps Fibre Channel speeds become available, higher-speed E_Ports for switch-to-switch uplinks are an obvious application.

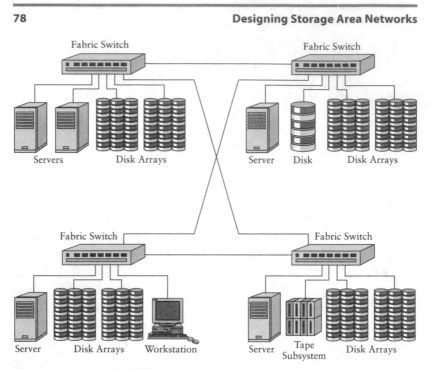

Figure 4-13 *A meshed fabric*

A complex fabric of multiple interconnected switches may be configured in a meshed topology, with alternative data paths from one N_Port to another through the fabric cloud, as depicted in Figure 4-13. Redundant paths through the fabric are desirable, since the failure of one path will allow traffic to be routed through alternative paths. As in the example cited previously, concurrently active alternative paths could result in out-of-order delivery of frames. A meshed fabric can avoid this problem by using **spanning tree**, an IEEE 802.1 standard commonly used in LAN bridges and routers. This protocol is used by network devices to determine optimum routes through a network and to hold redundant links in reserve. Alternative paths are activated only when a primary path fails. Spanning tree thus avoids duplication of active paths through the network and, in the case of a meshed fabric topology, allows in-order delivery of frames.

Because they must support N_Ports, public Arbitrated Loop, and switch-to-switch interconnect, fabrics are considerably more complex than are loop hubs. This is reflected in the per port cost of fabrics versus hubs, although competition and the introduction of efficient ASIC technology are driving the per port cost down. Considering that fabrics and loop hubs sometimes tie hundreds of thousands of dollars worth of servers and storage together and that these systems support the business of entire enterprises, Fibre Channel interconnect products are the least-expensive component of any storage network.

Fabrics provide a number of services that rationalize activity on the transport and facilitate adds, moves, and changes of attached devices. Fabric login services allow N_Ports and public loop NL_Ports to register with the fabric for communication. Simple Name Server functions streamline the process of discovery between communicating ports. And State Change Notification allows all fabric devices to keep current with topology changes caused by the introduction or removal of devices.

4.3.1 Fabric Login

When a fabric-capable Fibre Channel node is attached to a fabric switch, the node will perform **fabric login**, or **FLOGI**. Like port login, FLOGI is an extended link service command that establishes a session between two participants. In the case of FLOGI, an association, or login session, is created between the N_Port or public loop NL_Port and the switch. An N_Port sends a FLOGI frame containing its Node Name, N_Port Name (World-Wide Name), and service parameters to a well-known address of xFFFFFE. A public loop NL_Port first opens the destination AL_PA x00 before issuing its FLOGI request. In both cases, the login handler in the switch (at address xFFFFFE) accepts login by returning an accept (ACC) frame to the sender. If the fabric does not support certain service parameters requested by the N_Port or the NL_Port, it will set bits in the ACC frame to indicate as much.

An N_Port uses a 24-bit port address of x000000 when it logs in to the fabric. This allows the fabric to assign the appropriate port address to the device, based on the domain/area/port address format. The newly assigned address is contained in the destination (D_ID) field of the ACC response.

A similar process is used for a public loop NL_Port, except that the least-significant byte is used to assign an AL_PA, and the upper 2 bytes constitute a fabric loop identifier. Since the NL_Port had just previously emerged from a loop initialization (LIP) process prior to performing fabric login, it will already have a previously derived AL_PA.

It is up to the fabric to determine whether it will accept this AL_PA. If not, a new AL_PA is assigned to the NL_Port, which will cause it to launch another LIP process on its local loop segment. This ensures that the fabric-assigned AL_PA does not conflict with any previously selected AL_PAs on the loop. During the subsequent loop initialization sequence, the NL_Port will now have a fabric-assigned address it can select during the LIFA phase.

It should not be assumed that all host bus adapters, Fibre Channel disks, controllers, and so on, support fabric login or that various vendors' implementations are fully compatible. A large installed base of nonfabric Fibre Channel products were engineered for point-to-point or private loop configurations. As SANs have entered mainstream enterprise networks, however, pressure has been put on all vendors to supply fabric services so that more complex, high-bandwidth configurations can be built. Some of this pressure has been applied by the switch manufacturers themselves, which clearly have a vested interest in widespread adoption of fabrics. Interoperability, on the other hand, is being driven by a consortium of Fibre Channel vendors and dominant customers who have taken to heart the demise of proprietary network solutions.

4.3.2 Simple Name Server

As we saw in the discussion of Arbitrated Loop, initiators on the loop begin the process of target discovery by performing port logins to all 126 AL_PA device addresses. At gigabit speeds, this process occurs fairly quickly and allows each server to find target disks whenever a topology change occurs.

This process is untenable in fabric environments, since the potential address space is more than 15½ million addresses. Even at gigabit speeds, this would take some time. Fabrics rationalize the process of device discovery by providing a **Name Server** function in each switch. The Name Server is a database of objects that allows each fabric-attached device to register or query useful information, including name, address, and class of service capability of other participants. To keep the database compact, some objects, such as the type of FC-4 protocols supported by a registrant, are coded into a positional bit map.

The Name Server is accessed by performing a port login (PLOGI) to a well-known address of xFFFFFC. An N_Port or public NL_Port registers with the Name Server after performing PLOGI to it and then terminates the session. The device may register values for some or all of the database objects, but the most useful are its 24-bit port address, 64-bit Port Name, 64-bit Node Name, class of service parameters, FC-4 protocols supported, and port type, such as N or NL. Devices that support IP may also register their IPv4 or IPv6 IP addresses. Because the Name Server contains a table of both 24-bit addresses and the corresponding 64-bit World-Wide Names, one device can find another, based on either category.

The fabric Name Server makes it possible for a file server, for example, to begin discovering disk targets by inquiring for a list of all port addresses registered with the switch. This would relieve the file server from polling through 15½ million addresses. The file server could then perform PLOGIs with each reported address to discover, via upper-layer commands, which devices were SCSI-3 targets. Alternatively, since the Name Server also contains information on FC-4 protocol support, the file server could PLOGI only those port addresses that reported SCSI-3 support.

One area still under construction for Name Server functionality is the exchange of Name Server objects between fabrics, particularly between various vendors' implementations of fabrics. This does not pose a significant engineering challenge but will be required for extended enterprise configurations. Allowing any device on an extended fabric to discover and begin operations with any other device quickly is a prerequisite for implementing large SANs.

4.3.3 State Change Notification

Since fabrics are dynamic environments and may undergo topology changes as new devices are attached or previously active devices are taken off line, it is useful if notification of changes can be provided to other participants. This function is provided by **State Change Notification (SCN)** and a variant, **Registered State Change Notification (RSCN)**. SCN and RSCN are voluntary functions, in that an N_Port or an NL_Port must register its interest in being notified of network changes if another device alters state.

The original SCN service allowed an N_Port to send a change notification directly to another N_Port. RSCN does not allow this, since a direct N_Port–to–N_Port notification would not be seen by the remainder of the registrants. As a fabric service, RSCN allows all devices that have registered for notification to be informed if a topology change occurs. The type of change that is most meaningful for participants is when a device with which they have been communicating disappears from the fabric: powered off or removed. Servers, in particular, would want to be notified when resources were no longer available or when new resources have been added. Change notification thus provides for fabrics a function that loop initialization intrinsically provides for Arbitrated Loop.

4.3.4 Private Loop Support

Fabrics support public Arbitrated Loop devices via FL_Ports. The FL_Port has the highest-priority AL_PA, x00, always wins arbitration, is always temporary loop master during loop initialization, and provides the interface between the loop segment and the rest of the fabric. To communicate in a fabric environment, however, loop devices must be fabric-capable, that is, must perform fabric login following loop initialization.

Fibre Channel standards do not provide support for private, non-fabric loop devices on a fabric topology. This has not prevented fabric vendors, however, from devising means to accommodate the large population of private loop devices in the market. Allowing private loop–only NL_Ports to participate in a switched topology has obvious benefits for storage networks, which have been steadily deploying Arbitrated Loops over the past several years. Although upgrading a file server with a fabric-capable HBA is quite affordable, performing a forklift upgrade on very expensive disk arrays is not. Finding a means to incorporate these resources into a fabric is therefore a very attractive option.

Private loop support on a switch implies additional intelligence to monitor the activity of the private loop devices and to ensure that the existence of the fabric is transparent to them. Because the private loop devices are unaware of the fabric's presence, private loop support on a switch is sometimes described as **stealth,** or phantom, mode. Various implementations are available.

A segmentation strategy allows private loop devices to be dispersed on specific fabric ports, as shown in Figure 4-14. Although the total

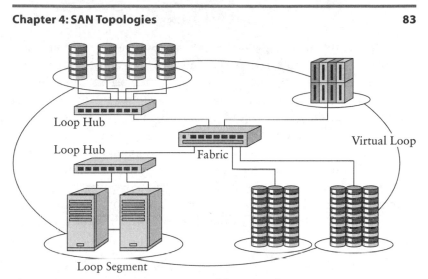

Figure 4-14 *Private loop support on a fabric switch*

number of private loop devices on a single port may be restricted by the vendor, the allocation of devices per port is usually determined by bandwidth and traffic considerations. Servers, for example, could be assigned to a single 100MBps port each, with large JBODs, representing multiple AL_PAs, assigned to other, full-bandwidth ports. What was previously a single, continuously shared transport would thus be segmented into a series of smaller 100MBps loops, some of which would have only one NL Port per loop. Segmentation transforms what was previously a physical Arbitrated Loop into a **virtual** Arbitrated Loop. Since the private loop devices are unaware of the fabric, they would arbitrate, open, transfer, and close transactions as before. A server, for example, would arbitrate for access as usual, but, because it is the only node on that loop segment, it would have no contenders and would immediately win. As it issues frames to a destination AL_PA, the switch logic intervenes and routes the frame directly to the switch port on which that AL_PA resides. By this means, segmentation provides the high-speed bandwidth of a fabric, without requiring fabric support. Segmentation also allows multiple conversations to occur simultaneously on the same virtual loop.

A translational strategy allows private loop devices to communicate with fabric-capable devices. This may be accomplished by manipulating the upper 2 bytes, or loop identifier, of the private loop device's port address. On the private loop segment, the loop identifier is x0000, indicating that the device is nonfabric. At the FL_Port, the fabric can proxy a loop identifier on behalf of the private loop device, which allows fabric-capable devices to address it. This manipulation implies a passive role for the private loop device, since it would require considerable overhead to allow private loop servers to discover and to communicate with fabric-capable storage. Translational private loop support is thus better suited to the access of private loop storage by fabric-capable servers.

4.3.5 Fabric Zoning

Fabric zoning allows the segregation of devices based on function, departmental separation, or potential conflicts between operating systems. Windows NT's habit of claiming all available storage resources, for example, makes isolation of UNIX storage from NT storage very desirable. Without some means of separating resources, putting marketing information and engineering on the same fabric might inadvertently give engineers a peek at the overly aggressive plans of marketing managers. Zoning resolves these potential problems by assigning devices or ports to separate zones or groups, enforcing separation via selective switching.

Zoning may be implemented on a port-by-port basis, which provides greater security, or by 24-bit port address or 64-bit World-Wide Name. The latter variation usually requires a dedicated server to configure and to maintain discrete assignment of subgroups. Port-based zoning is less involved, since assigning ports to one or more zones can be maintained by filtering logic in the routing engine.

A classic application for zoning is tape backup for heterogeneous operating systems, as illustrated in Figure 4-15. Windows NT servers and storage can be assigned to, say, zone A, whereas Sun Solaris servers and storage can be assigned to zone B. This segregation prevents NT from accessing the Sun storage arrays. Both NT and Solaris servers, however, could be assigned to a common zone C, which would include the tape subsystem. The third zone would allow both servers to back up or to restore from tape.

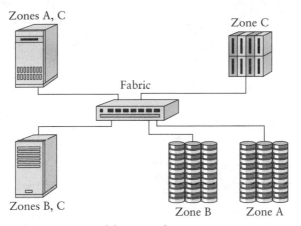

Figure 4-15 *Port zoning on a fabric switch*

4.4 Building Extended SANs

As SANs proliferate in enterprise networks, fabrics composed of multiple switches will become more commonplace. Showcase applications, such as full-motion video editing and high-performance relational database servers, are already driving large fabric configurations. Extended fabrics built for disaster-recovery applications already use multiple switches separated by long fiber-optic runs. The scalability that Fibre Channel promises is being challenged with every step of the technology's adoption, forcing standards to prove themselves in workable products.

Not all storage requirements, however, can be satisfied with fabrics alone. For some applications, the 100MBps per port and advanced fabric services are overkill and amount to wasted bandwidth and unnecessary cost. Marketing material of fabric vendors aside, proper design of SANs should be based on real application requirements. Fabrics facilitate this design goal, since they support both switched 100MBps and shared 100MBps topologies. As we will see in the case studies (Chapter 8), large enterprise SANs are typically constructed with a combination of fabric switches and Arbitrated Loops. These configurations allow bandwidth to be allocated as necessary, without

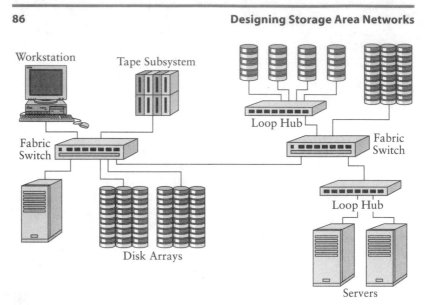

Figure 4-16 *Loop hubs and fabric switches in an extended configuration*

limiting growth or flexibility in expanding the storage network. See Figure 4-16.

4.5 Summary

Point to Point

- Point-to-point Fibre Channel is a dedicated connection between two N_Ports, typically a server and a disk.

Arbitrated Loop

- Arbitrated Loop is a ring topology supporting up to 127 attachments on a shared, 100MBps bandwidth.

- Loop hubs collapse the ring topology into a physical star configuration.

- Arbitrated Loop physical addresses (AL_PAs) are dynamically assigned, 1-byte identifiers.

- Loop initialization ensures that all devices have unique AL_PAs.

- Following loop initialization, initiators (servers) discover targets (disks) via port login.

- The Loop Port State Machine monitors activity on the loop and is responsible for initialization and loop access.

- Access to the loop is gained through arbitration. A fairness algorithm ensures that all participants are allowed utilization of the loop.

- Arbitrated Loop is nonbroadcast; the recipient of frames removes them from the loop.

- Total loop population should be application-driven.

- Private loop devices do not support fabric services; public loop devices will attempt fabric login to obtain a loop identifier.

- Loops support 10-kilometer links, but any long haul will incur propagation delay for all loop transactions.

- Managed loop hubs should be used for mission-critical environments.

- Redundant loops provide duplicate data paths and hardware for failover.

Fabrics

- A fabric is one or more Fibre Channel switches; each fabric port provides 100MBps bandwidth.

- Fabric addressing allows for more than 15 million unique identifiers.

- The 3-byte port address is divided into Domain, Area, and Port.

- Fabrics may be configured in a meshed topology to provide redundant links.

- An N_Port performs fabric login to establish a session with the fabric switch.

- An N_Port may register its World-Wide Name and service parameters with the Simple Name Server to facilitate discovery of targets.

- Registered State Change Notification allows a device to be notified if a communicating partner leaves or reenters the fabric.

- Some fabric switches may provide support for private loop devices and may allow public devices to access them.

- Zoning allows segregation of devices by port or World-Wide Name.

- Fabrics and loop hubs may be combined to create extended SANs.

Fibre Channel Products

The SAN landscape is being drawn with a variety of hardware and software product lines that both complement one another and compete for space in the storage-solutions market. The manufacturers of Fibre Channel products go to market along various paths, including large OEM (original equipment manufacturer) contracts with solutions providers, such as Compaq, Dell, HP, IBM, NCR, and Sun; arrangements with VAR (value-added reseller) and reseller channels, and through direct sales to corporate accounts. Some manufacturers produce only one part of the SAN solution, for example, Fibre Channel fabrics. Others engineer and manufacture a wider array of interconnect products, including loop hubs, fabrics, and transceivers.

Closer cooperation among noncompeting vendors, such as HBA manufacturers and hub or switch manufacturers, has promoted interoperability among the essential components of a SAN interconnect. Additionally, a few vendors have made substantial investments in their own verification labs to ensure that their products will play well with others. Interoperability of Fibre Channel products has also been encouraged by the Fibre Channel Loop Community, which includes vendors and interested end users. For the past several years, the University of New Hampshire (UNH) and Interphase Corporation have sponsored "plug fests" to test interoperability of Fibre Channel components. UNH formulates the test methodologies, and Interphase provides the lab facilities. Under a massive, mutual nondisclosure agreement, vendors may bring their latest products and microcode versions to test with other vendors' products. In addition to UNH, the University of Minnesota's Computational Science and Engineering Lab and a private facility, Medusa Labs, conduct ongoing tests of Fibre Channel products. These efforts discourage proprietary implementations and promote stability and confidence in Fibre Channel technology.

The spectrum of hardware components extends from GBICs to enterprise-level fabric switches. Transceivers, HBAs, loop hubs, switching hubs, and fabrics interconnect Fibre Channel–enabled RAIDs, JBODs, Fibre Channel–to–SCSI bridges, and native Fibre Channel tape subsystems. Software components include device drivers that are supplied with HBAs, SNMP (Simple Network Management Protocol), and Java management software for hubs and switches, file and volume management applications, failover software, and SAN-ready tape-backup applications. These hardware and software categories will be discussed later, but since the Fibre Channel market, like other markets, is subject to mergers and acquisitions and change in vendor identity, the emphasis will be on the useful features of each product type, not on the vendor responsible. In selecting particular products, the SAN designer should conduct the usual inquisition to grill vendors on their product features and functionality. A list of vendors and corresponding product categories is given in Appendix B.

5.1 Gigabit Interface Converters (GBICs)

Gigabit interface converters, or GBICs, are the most commonly used transceivers for Fibre Channel applications. GBICs provide flexibility for configuring various media and so are used by all major vendors of loop hubs, switching hubs, and fabric switches. The selection of GBICs for SAN interconnect is as important as the selection of loop hubs or fabric switches themselves, since without signal integrity at the link level, no higher functions can be performed.

First-generation optical GBICs used edge-emitting CD (compact disc) lasers, laser components normally used in consumer CD products. For high-speed data transport, only the highest-quality CD lasers could be used. Wafer manufacturing techniques for CD lasers require separation of the discrete components for testing to ensure quality, which contributes to manufacturing overhead and cost. In addition, CD lasers consume more power, radiate more heat, and are more susceptible to loss of calibration over time. These inherent problems of CD technology encouraged the development of alternative laser production, in particular, Vertical Cavity Surface Emitting Lasers, or VCSELs.

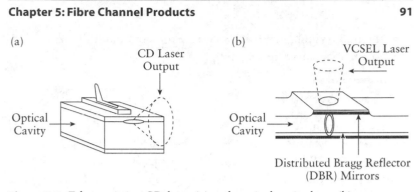

Figure 5-1 *Edge-emitting CD laser (a) and vertical cavity laser (b) components*

VCSEL laser technology has been in development for some time, awaiting resolution of obstacles to mass production. In the past few years, these problems have been solved one by one, allowing manufacture and packaging of a second-generation laser product and, for Fibre Channel applications, manufacture of second-generation GBICs. Unlike edge emitting CD lasers, vertical cavity lasers emit light perpendicular to the surface of the wafer substrate, as shown in Figure 5-1. VCSEL lasers also consume less power, radiate less heat, and maintain calibration better than their CD cousins do. And, since VCSEL lasers can be tested at the wafer, as opposed to discrete component level, manufacturing and quality testing can be performed more efficiently. GBIC manufacturers have converted from CD to VCSEL lasers, which helps ensure that these physical-layer components will maintain calibration and therefore data integrity at the system level.

Another advance in GBIC technology is the fulfillment of Serial ID functionality. Originally a voluntary feature of the GBIC specification, Serial ID has been engineered into second-generation products to provide a higher level of management at the physical layer. Serial ID allows a supporting enclosure, such as a hub, a switch or an HBA, to query the GBIC for inventory or status information. Inventory information includes manufacturer, date of manufacture, serial number, speed, media and lengths supported, and other useful tracking information. Depending on the vendor, status information may include current power consumption, output, and diagnostic data. Serial ID relies on the supporting enclosure to solicit this information, which implies that the hub, switch, or HBA can query the GBIC and report its findings to a management application.

5.2 Host Bus Adapters

Fibre Channel host bus adapters provide the interface between the server or workstation internal bus architecture and the external storage network. HBAs are available for various bus types and physical connections to the transport. Most commonly used are HBAs with PCI (Peripheral Component Interface) bus interfaces and shortwave fiber-optic transceivers. HBAs are supplied with software drivers for various operating system and upper-layer protocol support, as well as support for private loop, public loop, and fabric topologies. The installed base of HBAs is populated mainly with private loop attachment and SCSI-3 upper-layer protocol drivers. HBA vendors are also shipping fabric-capable products as the demand for switched SANs has increased.

Although the majority of HBAs have a single transceiver for connection to the SAN, some dual-ported and even quad-ported HBAs exist. As discussed in Chapter 4, these multiported devices would appear as a single Fibre Channel node containing two or more N_Ports, each with a unique World-Wide Name (Port_Name) and 24-bit port address. Multiported HBAs save bus slots by aggregating N_Ports but also pose a potential single point of failure should the HBA hang. Most HBAs offer a single Fibre Channel port, requiring additional HBAs to be installed if multiple links to the same or different SAN segment is desired.

The HBA embodies all four Fibre Channel layers, FC-0 through FC-4. At the FC-0 layer, the HBA has transmit and receive functions to connect to the link physically. For fiber optics, this connector is a GBIC, GLM, or 1×9 transceiver with standard dual SC coupling. For copper interface, the connector is DB-9 with four active wires or the HSSDC form factor. Behind the link interface, clock and data recovery (CDR) circuitry, serializing/deserializing functions, and an elasticity buffer and retiming circuit enable the receipt and transmission of gigabit serial data. Some of these FC-0 functions may be integrated onto a GLM in some cards, but as GBICs and 1×9s are more commonly used, the link-support circuitry is embedded on the HBA card.

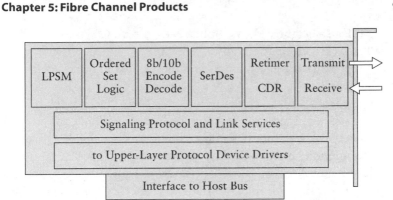

Figure 5-2 *Host bus adapter functional diagram*

The FC-1 transmission protocol requirements are met with on-board 8b/10b encoding logic for outbound data and decoding logic for incoming data, as well as low-level link management, flow control, and error-monitoring functions. For loop-capable HBAs, the FC-1 functions must be followed by a Loop Port State Machine (LPSM) circuit, typically included with other features in a single chip, such as Tachyon or Emulex Firefly. Above the LPSM, the HBA provides the signaling protocol for frame segmentation and reassembly, class of service, and credit algorithms, as well as link services for fabric and port login required by FC-2. At the FC-4 upper-layer protocol mapping level, the majority of HBAs provide SCSI-3 and IP software drivers for NT, UNIX, or MacOS operating systems.

How many of these functions are consolidated into one or a few chips is vendor-dependent, but the newer HBAs are ASIC-based and collapse most functions into an integrated architecture (see Figure 5-2). This has helped bring the cost down and provides more functionality on less real estate.

The rapid evolution of server technology to multiprocessor architectures and wider buses has also affected the development of HBAs. The 32-bit PCI bus found in some NT, UNIX and Mac platforms is capable of sustaining 132MBps throughput. Two 32-bit HBAs driving 100MBps each would outperform the bus. Newer, 64-bit PCI bus implementations, however, can drive 264MBps, permitting full utilization of two 64-bit PCI HBAs, providing that the HBAs could support full 100MBps sustained throughput. The 64-bit PCI HBAs are normally backward compatible with 32-bit buses, which provide more flexibility in sourcing and maintaining these cards in mixed-platform environments.

The design of HBAs typically includes flash memory for microcode. This is an important feature, since compatibility issues and microcode fixes are a fact of life for all network products. Having a means to upgrade microcode via a software utility is very useful and extends the life of the product. Device drivers for specific operating systems are also upgradeable. Installing new microcode or device drivers will, in most cases, require taking an HBA off line, which is additional incentive for redundant configurations in high-availability networks.

Since the majority of SANs in use are based on private Arbitrated Loop, HBA vendors have significant real-world experience—both positive and negative—with loop protocol and interoperability issues. Vendors have had to address link-level problems, loop initialization and arbitration issues, and compatibility conflicts when HBAs from multiple vendors are installed in the same server. For private loop configurations, most of these problems have been resolved.

At the same time, the demand for public loop support and fabric services adds complexity to HBA design, requiring additional microcode and memory to accommodate the potentially much higher population of communicators on a fabric topology. The first implementations of public loop and fabric services on HBAs have been engineered for fairly closed systems, such as a single fabric switch supplied by one vendor and a limited number of HBAs supplied by another. In some instances, the fabric vendor has assumed the task of writing fabric-specific device drivers for the HBA. The emphasis now, however, is on development for open systems environments, which encourages HBA vendors to engineer for generic, standards-based support for private loop, public loop, and point-to-point fabric attachment on a single card.

The SCSI-3 device driver supplied by the HBA vendor is responsible for mapping Fibre Channel storage resources to the SCSI bus/target/LUN triad required by the operating system (OS). These SCSI address assignments may be configured by operating system utilities and/or by a graphical interface supplied by the manufacturer. Since Fibre Channel addresses are self-configuring, the mapping between port addresses or AL_PAs, which may change, and the upper-layer SCSI device designations, which generally do not, is maintained by the HBA and its device driver interface to the OS.

Device drivers for IP must perform a similar function via the Address Resolution Protocol, or ARP. As upper-layer applications send data addressed to an IP destination, the HBA's device driver must resolve IP addresses into Fibre Channel addresses. Most configurations assume that all IP-attached devices reside on the same IP subnet and that no IP router engine exists in the fabric to which they are connected. If a SAN design requires concurrent use of IP and SCSI-3, some vendors require a separate card for each protocol. Others provide integrated SCSI-3 and IP support so that a single HBA can be used.

The trend in HBA development, as with other Fibre Channel products, is toward more sophisticated functionality at a reduced cost. Some host bus adapters offer add-on features, such as HBA-based RAID, which offloads the task of striping of data across multiple drives from the server's CPU (central processing unit). Support for the Virtual Interface (VI) protocol is also being developed. VI drivers will allow applications ready access to the Fibre Channel transport, without passing through traditional, CPU-intensive protocol stacks. And advanced diagnostic features, including SCSI Enclosure Services (SES) emulation, will allow HBAs to participate in umbrella SAN management platforms. Such enhanced features should be considered when querying HBA vendors about their product roadmaps and cooperative development efforts with other Fibre Channel suppliers.

5.3 Fibre Channel RAID

Redundant Arrays of Independent Disks, or RAIDs, are a well-established technology in traditional storage applications. RAID standards define methods for storing data to multiple disks and imply intelligence in the form of a RAID controller. The controller can be implemented in software, such as an application running on a file server, but is typically a dedicated card installed in a RAID storage enclosure. RAID storage configurations may include eight to ten disks for a departmental-level array or, for enterprise applications, many more.

When a server is connected to a single disk drive, reads or writes of multiple data blocks are limited by the buffering capability and rotation speed of the disk. While the disk is busy processing one or more blocks, the host must wait for acknowledgment before sending or receiving more. Throughput can be increased by dispersing data blocks across several disks in a RAID, a technique called **striping**. In a write operation, for example, the host can send fewer data blocks to multiple targets consecutively and avoid swamping the capacity of any individual drive. This simplified RAID is called **level 0** and, although boosting performance, it does not provide data security. If a single disk fails, data cannot be reconstructed from the survivors.

Other RAID levels introduce data integrity by either writing parity data to a dedicated drive or writing parity information on each drive in an array. RAID **level 3** writes byte-level parity to a dedicated drive. RAID **level 4** writes block-level parity to a parity drive. Since a dedicated drive contains the information required to reconstruct data, levels 3 and 4 pose a security problem if one of the data drives and the parity drive itself fail. RAID **level 5** addresses this problem by striping block-level parity information across each drive. If an individual drive fails, it can be reconstructed from the parity information contained on the other drives. Another technique, **level 1**, achieves full data security by sacrificing the performance gain of striping in favor of simple disk mirroring. In disk mirroring, every write operation to a primary disk is duplicated on a secondary, or mirrored, disk. If the primary disk fails, the server can switch over to the backup disk. Some RAID techniques may be combined, as in **level 0+1**, to provide both striping throughput and data redundancy via mirroring, as shown in Figure 5-3.

All RAID levels assume that the disks in a redundant array have the same storage capacity in terms of megabytes. The smallest drive in an array determines the usable disk space of all other drives, so introducing a larger drive does not increase the available storage. The same is true of spindle rotation speed, since the slowest performer will determine the available throughput. RAID enclosures, therefore, are populated with the same drive type per set and typically include unused hot spares that can be brought on line if a drive fails.

The various techniques that RAID provides for redundancy and speed may be implemented either by a dedicated RAID controller housed in the same enclosure as the disks or by a RAID controller provisioned in the host system or file server. Data is passed from the operating system to the RAID controller, which then manages the striping

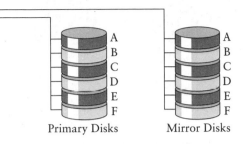

Blocks ABCDEF of a Single Data File

Figure 5-3 *RAID 0+1 striping plus mirroring*

or mirroring tasks. If the operating system manages data striping or mirroring, the host CPU must devote cycles to these tasks. The latter technique is called **software RAID.** In the next section, we will see how software RAID is implemented on JBODs.

Fibre Channel–attached RAID enclosures use an integrated RAID controller that sits behind the Fibre Channel interface (Figure 5-4). The RAID controller receives SCSI-3 requests via the loop or fabric and stores or retrieves data from the array, using the appropriate RAID levels. From the standpoint of the Fibre Channel interconnect, the physical interface between the RAID controller and its disks is irrelevant. The RAID controller appears as an N_Port or an NL_Port to the outside world but may use a proprietary bus, a SCSI bus, or other architecture to talk to its drives. For performance and reliability, however, RAID manufacturers may also incorporate Fibre Channel technology *behind* the RAID controller. This allows the use of Fibre Channel drives and the redundant topologies that, for example, dual-loop configurations provide. The use of Arbitrated Loop between the RAID controller and its Fibre Channel disks is invisible to the SAN, since the RAID controller still appears as a single N_Port or NL_Port to the rest of the topology.

Since a Fibre Channel RAID controller must support the functionality of an HBA and independent intelligence to manage striping and mirroring functions, it brings additional cost to a storage solution. Fibre Channel RAID products justify the additional expense by including high-availability and storage management features required for enterprise networking. RAID enclosures offer redundant, hot-swappable

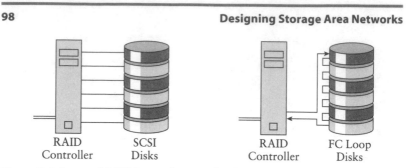

Figure 5-4 *Internal SCSI bus and internal Arbitrated Loop RAID*

power supplies, redundant fans, and self-diagnostics. Most accommodate on-line spare drives for autoreconstruction of data if a disk failure
occurs. Large systems can be scaled to hundreds of gigabytes, to more
than a terabyte of storage, which implies an enterprise-level budget.

For mission-critical SANs, Fibre Channel RAIDs offer a number of
advantages. The advanced diagnostics support, management features,
reliability, and scalability typical of such high-end systems fill in most
of the check boxes for enterprise storage selection criteria. Server processing resources benefit by offloading data redundancy tasks to the
RAID controller. Additionally, when the server is freed from the overhead of software RAID, the server is also liberated from exclusive
ownership of the storage device. Since no single server is responsible
for managing the striping of data to multiple disks, any server may
own part or all of the RAID controller's data. Fibre channel RAID thus
enables server clustering and other applications that are predicated on
co-ownership of storage resources.

From a SAN design standpoint, Fibre Channel RAIDs simplify
configurations, since the RAID controller appears as a single port
address to the loop or fabric. Adding drives to a RAID enclosure does
not add to the population of the SAN transport, even if the RAID
enclosure internally uses Arbitrated Loop to access its disks. For Arbitrated Loops, attachment of more than a terabyte of storage is possible
without consuming all available AL_PAs. For direct fabric attachment,
the RAID controller and all of its storage appear as a single N_Port on
its own 100MBps segment, whereas a single JBOD enclosure will
appear as multiple NL_Ports sharing a common bandwidth. JBODs do
have one distinct advantage over RAIDs, however: cost.

5.4 Fibre Channel JBODs

A JBOD, or just a bunch of disks, is an enclosure with multiple Fibre Channel disk drives inserted into a common backplane. The backplane provides the transmit-to-receive connections that bring the assembled drives into a common Arbitrated Loop segment and bypass electronics that enable drives to be inserted or removed without disrupting the loop circuit. Since Fibre Channel drives provide primary and secondary NL_Ports for dual-loop attachment, the JBOD enclosure typically includes external interfaces for connecting two loops, as shown in Figure 5-5.

A JBOD brings the receive lead going to the first drive of a set and the transmit lead coming from the last drive of a set to a Fibre Channel interface, typically DB-9 copper. When the JBOD's interface is connected to a fibre channel hub or switch, the connection is not to a single Fibre Channel device but to multiple independent loop devices within the enclosure. An eight-drive JBOD, for example, appears as eight AL_PAs to the interconnect. If the connection is made to a switch, the switch port must be an FL_Port, since the downstream enclosure is a loop segment. If the connection is to an Arbitrated Loop hub, the population of the entire loop is increased by the number of drives in the JBOD. JBODs, unlike Fibre Channel RAIDs, have a direct impact on the topology to which they're attached.

Some JBOD-based disk arrays incorporate additional logic for enclosure management, usually a Fibre Channel controller that supports SCSI Enclosure Services (SES) queries. This adds to the configuration additional AL_PA, which can be addressed by an SES management

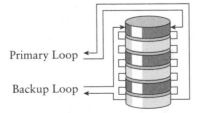

Primary Loop

Backup Loop

Figure 5-5 *JBOD disk configuration*

workstation to solicit power, temperature, and fan status. JBODs may also include options for configuring the backplane to support dual loops to a single set of drives or dividing the drives into separate smaller sets, with a single loop attachment each (see Figure 5-6).

How the individual disks within a JBOD are used for data is determined by a host server. Volume administration tools for the appropriate operating system are used to assign drives as individual logical disks or to assign a group of drives or the entire JBOD as a logical disk. In the latter case, software RAID can be used to increase performance and to provide redundancy. Use of software RAID, however, implies that the server will be the exclusive owner of the JBOD, since that server alone is responsible for managing striping of data across the drives. Even if another server sits on the SAN, it will have to request the JBOD's data via the external LAN. This problem has been addressed by custom application software on some systems, but it requires an additional server on the SAN to coordinate file information (metadata) management. Generally, software RAID on JBODs offers redundancy for dedicated server-to-storage relationships but does not lend itself to server clustering or serverless tape backup across the SAN.

Software RAID provides increased performance by avoiding the latency of reading or writing to a single drive, but this gain must be balanced with the increased traffic load on the loop. In a normal disk write operation to a single drive, for example, the server must first set up the write transaction with a SCSI-3 write command to the target. On an Arbitrated Loop, this may require several loop accesses (**tenancies** of the loop) before the disk is ready to accept data. The transfer of frames to the disk, in turn, is not normally accomplished with a single possession of the loop unless the file is fairly small. If the server is sending frames more quickly than the target can process them, the target will accept what it can and then close the loop. The loop must then be regained for each additional transfer of frames. A single write operation may therefore require multiple tenancies or loop occupations before all frames have been sent and a write response is sent by the target to the initiator.

This problem is aggravated by software RAID used with a JBOD, since the initiator must conduct a series of small transactions to multiple targets. At the SCSI-3 level, commands would queue to the targets and await response from each one before more frames could be sent.

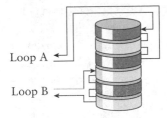

Loop A

Loop B

Figure 5-6 *Dividing the JBOD backplane into separate loops*

Even if the initiator can leverage transfer mode to address several targets during a single tenancy, it is still limited by disk performance and the timeout values of Arbitrated Loop. This incurs more protocol overhead and traffic on the loop, which may be a concern if the loop has other active initiators. A loop with four servers, each with its own loop-attached JBOD, would suffer much higher protocol overhead than a comparable configuration with loop-attached RAIDs.

JBOD enclosures are normally marketed with eight- to ten-drive bays, some of which may be configured for failover. Some very large disk arrays are packaged in 19-inch rack form factors, with more than twenty disks per JBOD module and up to four modules per rack enclosure. These high-end systems may include rack-mounted Arbitrated Loop hubs or switches for connecting JBOD modules to one another and to servers for single- or dual-loop configurations. Given the amount of customer data that is stored on such arrays, managed hubs or fabric switches are preferable to unmanaged interconnects. Dual power supplies, redundant fans, and SES management options allow JBODs to be used in high-availability environments. Vendors may also provide an upgrade path to add a RAID controller card to the enclosure, which extends the life of the original investment. The customer can begin with a partially populated JBOD enclosure and add disks as storage needs dictate. A RAID controller option can then be added to increase performance and to offload software RAID tasks from the host.

5.5 Arbitrated Loop Hubs

Fibre Channel hubs continue to be a popular choice for SAN implementations, due primarily to their ease of installation and lower per port cost versus fabrics. Hubs are available from a number of vendors in various port configurations, interface types, and levels of management. Unlike other Fibre Channel devices, a hub is a passive participant in the SAN topology. Except for special management functions that may be provided by a vendor, a hub normally has no port address. So although all loop traffic passes through the hub, no NL_Port speaks directly to the hub. Finding a means to maintain this nonintrusive role and yet engineer advanced management features into hub technology is a challenge all hub vendors have assumed.

5.5.1 Star Topology for Arbitrated Loop

As discussed in Chapter 4, Arbitrated Loops can be wired into a ring by connecting the transmit lead of one device to the receive lead of another and extending this scheme until all devices are physically configured into a loop. This eliminates the cost of a concentrating hub but exposes the topology to considerable risk. If a connection fails anywhere along the ring, the entire loop goes down. Troubleshooting is complicated by the fact that there is no central point at which all cabling is brought together, and, since the loop is down, no in-band diagnostics, if available, could be used. In addition, introducing or removing an NL_Port to the configuration requires downing the loop for the duration of the change. Bringing a network down for an add, move, or change is not normally tolerated outside of test lab environments.

As illustrated in Figure 5-7, loop hubs simplify the cable plant by concentrating physical links at a central location and minimize disruption by providing bypass circuitry at each port. Each link in the physical loop is brought into the hub, which creates a star cabling configuration while maintaining the circular data path through all devices. Port-bypass circuitry automatically routes around any hub port that loses Fibre Channel signaling, which prevents a broken cable or a disabled NL_Port from disrupting loop operations.

Hubs are normally colocated with storage arrays or servers in 19-inch equipment racks, which offer a further convenience for verifying status and cabling within the enclosure. Large storage arrays may have multiple JBODs or RAIDs and multiple loop hubs configured into separate or redundant loops within a single 19-inch enclosure.

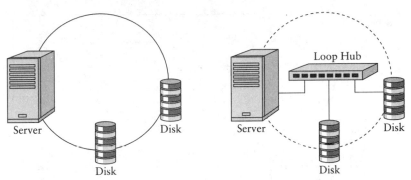

Figure 5-7 *Wiring concentration with an Arbitrated Loop hub*

5.5.2 Hub Architecture

Hub design varies from vendor to vendor, but all incorporate basic features specific to Arbitrated Loop. The hub embodies the loop topology by completing circuits through each port and then joining the transmit of the last port to the receive of the first. When cabling from an NL_Port is plugged into a hub port, the port must, at minimum, be able to recover valid Fibre Channel clock (1.0625 gigabaud). If the signaling is too fast—for example, inadvertently connecting a Gigabit Ethernet device at 1.25 gigabaud—or too slow, the port will remain in bypass mode. Depending on the sophistication of the loop hub, an insertion decision will be made on the basis of the received Fibre Channel signal or a combination of valid signal and valid ordered sets via protocol decode. For most unmanaged loop hubs, if the attached NL_Port is providing valid signal, the device is allowed to insert into the loop.

A port in bypass mode shunts the bit stream it has received from its upstream neighbor directly to its immediate downstream neighbor. If a device is removed from port 4, for example, the bypass circuitry will route traffic from port 3 to port 5. Port 4's transmitter, however, may still be active. Some vendor implementations turn off the transmitter as long as the port is in bypass mode. The transmitter is then enabled only when the hub port receives valid signal from a newly attached device. Other designs leave the transmitter on so that an attached device will immediately see valid Fibre Channel signal from the hub and thus insert without delay.

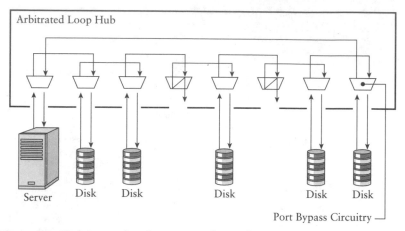

Figure 5-8 *Hub internal architecture with port bypass circuitry*

Autobypass circuitry allows the loop topology to self-configure as devices are added or removed (see Figure 5-8). This is an elementary feature of all hub architecture, not, despite some promotional material, a proprietary marketing advantage of any specific vendor. As servers or storage arrays are taken off line or reenabled, the circumference of the loop circuit automatically contracts or expands through the associated ports. At the link protocol level, loop initialization handles the automatic reconfiguration of port addresses to accommodate newly attached devices. The combination of hub autobypass and insertion with Arbitrated Loop's self-configuring addressing algorithm offloads tedious administration tasks from day-to-day storage network operations and facilitates changes to the topology, with minimal disruption to data traffic.

Loop hubs may offer one or more LEDs (light-emitting diodes) per port to display port status. Typically, two LEDs are provided: a green LED to indicate a link connection and an amber LED to indicate the current bypass mode. Depending on the vendor's specification, the combination of green and amber LED states can be used to display a number of port conditions, listed in Table 5-1. Some implementations use a single, multicolored LED per port, which reduces the number of diagnostic display states available. Port LEDs give the operator an at-a-glance status of a device's connection state and, by simplifying troubleshooting, help reduce down time.

Table 5-1   Hub Port LED State Table

Green	Amber	Port State
Off	Off	No device attached
On	Off	Device attached and loop inserted
On	On	Device attached and bypassed
Off	On	Bad GBIC; port bypassed
Blinking	Blinking	Maintenance mode via hub management

Hub architecture is not dictated by specific Fibre Channel standards other than the implied parameters established by Arbitrated Loop documents, such as FC-AL, FC-AL-2, and so on, and physical-layer FC-0 standards. As long as they do not violate Arbitrated Loop and Fibre Channel physical-layer provisions, vendors are free to engineer variations in port density, port type, signal processing, and management features to enhance functionality. Consequently, a variety of hub products are available that are engineered to various marketing requirements, from simple entry-level to enterprise-class configurations.

Port density on a single unit may vary from as few as 5 ports to as many as 32. The most common density is from 6 to 12 ports per unit. This range is adequate for most loop implementations, and, by cascading hubs together, higher loop populations can be achieved. Loop hubs are typically 1-U (one rack unit) high units, which allows, for example, up to 48 ports to be supplied in four slots of a 19-inch rack. Higher densities can be configured with some models but usually only by providing ports on both back and front of the hub chassis, thus complicating the cabling scheme.

Port types also vary from vendor to vendor. Fixed copper ports may be found on low-cost, entry-level loop hubs, although others in the same class offer GBIC-based ports. Fixed copper ports are not a highly desirable feature, since they are prone to higher EMI emissions and jitter. Cross-talk, or signaling from one port affecting its neighbor, is also a concern with copper interfaces. In addition, the lower price of fixed copper ports is offset by the extra cost of media interface adapters (MIAs) if the customer wishes to use fiber-optic cabling from the hub to a device. Most midrange and higher-end loop hubs use

GBIC-based ports, due to the flexibility GBICs offer for mixing copper, shortwave, and longwave media. This design allows the customer to provision ports as needed and to change from one media type to another without swapping out the hub. GBIC-based hubs may be marketed "without media," that is, without the additional cost of the GBICs themselves, or bundled with a specific configuration of optical and/or copper GBICs preinstalled. Since the majority of fabric switches also use GBICs, this hub architecture simplifies parts sparing for storage networks based on both fabrics and loops. When selecting GBIC-based products, however, it should not be assumed that all GBICs are created equal. Both copper and fiber-optic GBICs vary in quality from manufacturer to manufacturer, and since these components play a critical role in physical-layer transport, selection of the proper GBIC is an important part of hub selection.

Another variation in hub architecture is reflected by the vendor's implementation of port-level signal regeneration circuitry. In order for a hub port to validate the received Fibre Channel signal and thus make a bypass decision, it must recover the signal clock embedded in the incoming bit stream. To do this, a clock and data recovery circuit, or CDR, is required. If the signal is valid—is at 1.0625 gigabaud—the bit stream is regenerated and passed to the next downstream port. Hubs that use a synchronous repeater circuit use the recovered clock to regenerate the bit stream. Hubs that use retimers use an independent clock to regenerate the stream asynchronously. Both methods are valid techniques for signal handling, and both involve compromises between performance and signal quality.

A repeater-based design provides higher performance, since transit of the bit stream through the port encounters minimal delay. A well-designed repeater circuit may incur less than 30 nanoseconds port-to-port latency. A retimer, on the other hand, requires an elasticity buffer for signal processing and, like HBAs or other Fibre Channel ports, may incur more than 240 nanoseconds port-to-port delay. From a performance standpoint alone, an efficient repeater design is the preferred signaling strategy.

The repeater, however, is dependent on the inbound signal to generate its outbound clock. If the signal has suffered propagation delay or jitter in transit, a potential exists for jitter transference to the next port. How significant such accumulation is depends on the design of the repeater circuit. Some repeater circuits are very poor at jitter suppression; others are very good. A retiming circuit eliminates the issue of jitter accumulation completely by providing an independently timed signal on the outbound link. In terms of signal quality, a retimer is generally preferred over a repeater. In practice, however, the presence of a retimer at each hub port does not guarantee jitter-free signaling. Depending on the vendor's hardware design, a retiming port may still produce considerable jitter in the outbound signal if care is not taken to eliminate transients, noise from power supply sources, and other EMI sources on the circuit board or GBIC. For any technology involving gigabit speeds, there is no substitute for good electrical engineering.

In terms of hub-selection criteria, a datasheet review is not sufficient for deciding whether a repeater-based or a retimer-based product is more appropriate. When properly implemented, both circuits offer advantages. Some hub products with repeater-based architecture provide far better signal quality than do other products with retimers. A well-designed and executed retimer circuit is most advantageous when longwave (up to 10 kilometers) loop ports are required, since maximum Fibre Channel distances are the most vulnerable to timing jitter.

5.5.3 Unmanaged Hubs

Unmanaged hubs are frequently used for small, single-vendor environments that are less susceptible to the dynamics of larger, more complex SAN installations. If only a single server and one or two disk arrays are involved, there is less exposure to prolonged down time if a cable or other component fails. And if a single-solutions provider has supplied the server, HBA, disk arrays, hub, GBICs, and cabling, there is less demand for higher-level SAN diagnostics that a multivendor configuration would require.

Unmanaged hubs are a simple, low-cost, entry-level interconnect solution. They typically provide port-bypass circuitry, based on valid signaling alone, and port LEDs to display insertion or bypass status. If an attached device is unplugged or powered off, an unmanaged hub will autobypass the port and light the appropriate port LEDs. Having no intelligence or ordered-set recognition circuitry, an unmanaged hub cannot respond to protocol violations or conditions, such as a port streaming LIP(F8), which would bring the loop down. The selection of an unmanaged hub therefore implies an assumed risk. The trade-off for lower cost and simplified installation is the longer mean time to repair that might follow a loop failure.

Some very large, mission-critical SANs use unmanaged loop hubs, normally bundled by the solutions provider. These are often deployed in redundant loop configurations to provide an alternative path if a loop failure occurs. The lack of visibility to the hub and loop status via hub management is balanced against the security that redundant paths offer. Such implementations are, by and large, lower risk, since the hubs and other interconnect components rarely fail. The worst-case scenario for redundant, unmanaged loops would be the quiet failure of the backup loop, followed eventually by the failure of the primary loop. Without hub management to report the backup loop failure, the redundancy would no longer be in force, and the failure of the primary loop would bring the system down. Troubleshooting would then be complicated by the fact that what appeared as a single occurrence, that is, system failure, was the result of two separate events on two separate loop topologies.

Unmanaged hubs are a logical choice for low-cost storage network solutions in which economical servers and small JBODs are used to meet budget restraints. These entry-level systems bring high-performance SAN capability within reach of small business and departmental applications and create the initial infrastructure on which more sophisticated requirements can grow.

5.5.4 Managed Hubs

Managed hubs introduce intelligence into the SAN interconnect. The degree of intelligence and management capability varies from product to product and is normally reflected in price. At the low end of the managed hub offering, basic hub status and port controls are available via Web browser, TELNET, or SNMP management software. At the high end, advanced diagnostics and proactive management features are available on a variety of management platforms, including HP Open-View and Java-based applications.

Support for management functionality in Arbitrated Loop hubs has two basic components. First, at the hardware level, additional on-board circuitry is needed to monitor power supply, fan, temperature, and port status. These functions are the minimum requirement for hub management, although some implementations concentrate on port status alone. Managed hubs with advanced capabilities also provide more extensive diagnostic circuits to monitor the state of the loop, protocol activity, and more complete port and hub status. Second, for these circuits to be useful, the hub must be able to report to and accept commands from an external management workstation. This is typically accomplished via an Ethernet port on the hub, over which SNMP queries and commands are sent from an NT or a UNIX console. The application software used to manage a hub is provided by the hub vendor, either as a stand-alone program or as a utility launchable from more comprehensive SAN management applications.

Managed hub products that support SNMP or Web browsers can be managed from anywhere in an IP routed network (see Figure 5-9). This is a distinct advantage for customer support organizations and network command centers, as well as resellers or VARs having support contracts with remote customers. SNMP is preferable to browser-based management, since multiple hubs can be managed from a single workstation. Browser-based management typically speaks to only one IP address, and therefore to one hub, at a time. SNMP and other management protocols and strategies are discussed in more detail in Chapter 7.

The first managed hub products in the Fibre Channel market provided basic enclosure status, similar to the SCSI Enclosure Services (SES) that managed disk arrays and other storage products support.

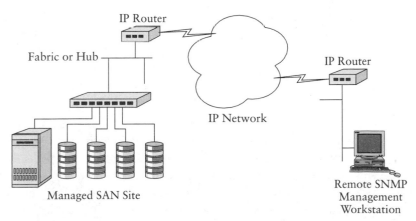

Figure 5.9 *Managed hub SAN with remote SNMP/IP management*

Basic enclosure status includes power, fan, and temperature monitoring, as well as port enable/disable controls. The vendor-supplied management application for the first-generation products graphically depicts the hub enclosure and, via menu selection, displays additional screens for hub and port status. Although it is important to be alerted if a fan or a power supply fails, these components generally have very high mean time between failure and are not the usual suspects when a loop problem occurs. For day-to-day storage network operation, protocol-related events, such as streaming LIP(F8) or failing to conclude initialization, have a higher statistical occurrence than do power supply or temperature issues.

Second-generation managed hub products have addressed this by incorporating ordered-set recognition into the management interface. By monitoring both the Fibre Channel signal and the data embedded within it, the managed hub can detect and act on protocol violations or conditions that would endanger the loop. The most obvious condition is presented by a device that is streaming LIP(F8)s onto the loop. If the managed hub can detect LIP(F8), it can automatically bypass the offending port. LIP(F8) autobypass elevates the hub's role from simple problem detection to problem isolation. If a harmful condition can be automatically isolated by the hub, the rest of the loop's transactions can continue operation. This is preferable to simply having the problem detected and reported and then relying on human intervention for correction. Some products also include automatic recovery features to ensure that all loop devices can regain normal operation if a loop failure occurs. Ordered set recognition and bypass policies based on protocol events are part of a growing set of **loop integrity** features that managed hub vendors, driven by their customers and market competition, are building into their products. Loop integrity functionality is a prerequisite for adoption of loop topology by enterprise networks with high-availability requirements.

At the high end of the managed hub market, ordered set recognition has been leveraged to provide additional features. It might be useful, for example, to put a hub port into bypass mode and to transmit ordered sets to a new disk array before it is inserted into the production loop. By monitoring the response from the attached device, it would be possible to verify the operation of the GBICs, cable plant, and array along both transmit and receive paths. The new disk array could then be brought on line without the risk that a faulty GBIC or cable would bring the loop down. In some products, ordered set recognition logic is used to provide protocol status on all ports. By displaying the ARBs, OPNs, IDLEs, and so on, observed at every port, protocol activity can reveal the current status of loop traffic. If a server, for example, cannot talk to a disk array, it is useful to know whether the server is properly arbitrating for access to the loop.

Additional managed hub features may include CRC error detection, link errors, invalid transmission words, most-active AL_PAs, loop status, and topology mapping. A loop status indicator is a valuable feature, because when troubleshooting a server or array problem, it is essential to know whether the network itself is up or down. Loop status may be displayed by an LED on the hub chassis and through the management graphical interface. Automatic topology mapping presents an interesting challenge, since it implies a much higher level of intelligence in the hub. To identify other hubs in a cascaded configuration and the devices attached to their respective ports, the managed hub would necessarily assume the role of an NL_Port to send and to receive SES queries over SCSI-3 protocol. Those results could then be reported to a management workstation responsible for drawing a coherent map of the configuration. Some implementations use a proprietary scheme to map cascaded hubs but lack the capability of identifying attached devices.

Most vendors provide an event log for automatic logging of hub and loop events. The event log may be queried from the hub, using TELNET or SNMP, or replicated on the management workstation for a permanent record of activity. An event log is a very useful diagnostic tool, especially for troubleshooting intermittent problems that may occur during unattended operation of the management workstation.

The graphical interfaces supplied with managed hubs vary in capability and platform support from vendor to vendor. At the low end, browser-based management may provide screens for basic port configuration and status but no active updates for visual cues on hub status. At the high end, NT or Java-based applications provide a "back of box" or portside depiction of the hub, with color-coded cues and legends for hub and port status. Pop-up alerts may be provided for significant events, as well as SNMP traps to send notification to another management platform. Depending on the customer's management philosophy, the location of a SAN management workstation may be colocated with the SAN or incorporated into a network operations center where LAN and WAN management is performed. Consequently, managed hub applications may provide additional interfaces to integrate into HP OpenView, Tivoli, or other comprehensive management platforms.

5.6 Switching Hubs

Switching hubs are a hybrid SAN solution, intermediate between hubs and fabrics. Similar to the functionality of private loop stealth or phantom mode for some fabric switches, switching hubs leverage the simplicity of Arbitrated Loop with the higher-performance bandwidth of switches. By design, switching hubs are not fabric-capable, thereby reducing the engineering requirements and additional cost associated with fabric switches. Switching hubs are therefore more expensive than standard loop hubs but are more economical than fabrics. For configurations that require high bandwidth but no more than 126 total devices, switching hubs offer a good price/performance solution.

Switching hubs typically provide six to eight ports, each of which supports 100MBps throughput. The attached loop nodes are configured into one virtual loop composed of multiple 100MBps loop segments. By assigning high-performance servers to their own ports and RAIDs or JBODs to other ports, switching hubs provide the aggregate bandwidth of fabric switches. The segmentation of one logical loop into smaller virtual loop segments also allows loop behavior to be modified. Loop initialization can be restricted to a single port, which removes a source of potential disruption for sensitive applications, such as streaming video or streaming tape backup. Additionally, concurrent conversations within a single virtual loop are now possible. A server on port 3, for example, could be accessing storage on port 7 while a server on port 1 could access data on port 6. Because normal loop protocols, such as ARBs or OPNs, and the data frames themselves do not have to traverse the entire loop, switching hubs also allow long hauls (up to 10 km) to be accommodated without impacting overall loop performance.

At the high end of the hub product offering, switching hubs support SNMP, SES, or other management features. Depending on the vendor's design, some products include advanced diagnostic features, including the ability to direct, via management interface, data-capture traffic on any other port without disrupting the topology.

5.7 Fabric Switches

The deployment of fabric switches was initially hindered by cost—more than $2,000 per port—and the requirement for fabric login services for host bus adapters and disk arrays. Cost reductions due to ASIC technology, as well as widespread support of fabric services by other Fibre Channel vendors, have moved fabric switches into the mainstream of SAN solutions and SAN solutions, in turn, into the mainstream of enterprise networking.

Switch products, like Arbitrated Loop hubs, provide basic features for the topology they support. All fabric switches support 100MBps per port, all provide a high-speed routing engine to switch frames from source to destination, and all provide basic services for fabric login and name server functions. Fortunately for the end-user base, vendor competition has also driven cooperation to ensure that fabric products abide by common standards. Vendor differentiation, then, centers on such vendor-specific issues as port density, performance, and value-added functionality for ease of installation and management.

Fabric switches may support 8 to 16 ports for departmental applications or 32 to 64 ports for larger enterprises. Cascading fabrics via expansion ports (E_Ports) allow small and medium configurations to expand as SAN requirements grow, with the caveat that each cascade consumes additional ports and that the expansion links themselves may become potential bottlenecks for fabric-to-fabric communication. Some switch products support multiple links between two switches with load balancing of traffic. This resolves the congestion issue but may introduce another problem if the source and destination N_Ports on either side have difficulty with out-of-order frame delivery. Another alternative for supporting higher populations is to devote one or more switches for switch interconnect, that is, a switch provisioned exclusively with E_Ports, as shown in Figure 5-10. This strategy is appropriate for evolving SANs in which the initial port requirements cannot justify the expense of a 32-port or 64-port enclosure.

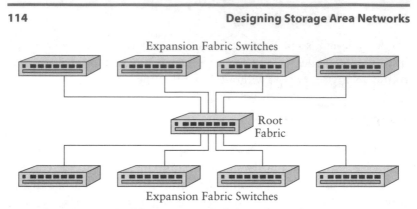

Figure 5-10 *Increasing fabric ports with dedicated switch interconnect*

Fibre Channel standards define F_Ports for attaching nodes (N_Ports), E_Ports for fabric expansion, G_Ports for supporting either N_Ports or other fabrics, and NL_Ports for loop attachment. The standards do not define how, specifically, these port types are to be implemented in hardware, so vendor designs may differ. Some products offer a modular approach, with separate port cards for each port type. Others provide ports that can be configured via management software or autoconfiguration to support any port type. The latter offers more flexibility for changing SAN topologies, permitting redistribution or addition of devices with minimal disruption. Even then, products may vary in the number of ports that can be concurrently configured for loop. Supporting loop devices requires more switch resources, and although some vendor implementations make no restrictions, others limit assigning ports as FL_Ports to as few as four.

Performance differences among fabric products are minimal when ASIC technology is used. Non-ASIC fabrics typically incur more than 2 microseconds latency per frame switch. ASIC-based fabrics normally incur less than 2 microseconds latency. As latency drops into the nanosecond range, the fabric is essentially performing at wire speed. Fabric performance is also affected by the transmit and receive buffering capability of each port. Some products provide sufficient buffering to queue 2 frames; others can queue 16 or more. Additional buffering allows the fabric to handle congestion without throwing away frames, which speeds the end-to-end communication between source and destination.

Enhanced functionality not covered by specific Fibre Channel standards also includes support for private loop devices, zoning, and fabric management. As discussed in Chapter 4, private loops on fabric switches may be implemented in several ways. A virtual private loop strategy allows private loop devices to communicate with one another as if they were on the same loop segment. The physical configuration, however, divides the loop population into smaller segments per switch port, which enables switching between private loop segments. Concurrent conversations on a single virtual loop, as well as the ability to restrict propagation of LIPs, makes virtual private loop attractive for installations that must support legacy, nonfabric loop devices. Translational private loop extends this support by allowing public N_Ports to communicate with private loop devices. A fabric-enabled server could, via translation, access private loop JBODs or RAIDs. As with FL_Port provisioning, the number of private loop devices and the number of switch ports devoted to private loop may differ from one product to another.

Almost all fabric switches support some zoning variation. Port zoning allows a port to be assigned to an exclusive group of other ports. In most implementations, a single port can be assigned to several groups, depending on application requirements. Port zoning is normally a no-cost enhancement to the switch and is an accessible means to segregate servers and their storage from other servers or to isolate various departments sharing the same switch resource. Other zoning options include zoning by Port World-Wide Name. This more granular approach offers more flexibility in assigning zones but also incurs more cost. Zoning on World-Wide Names may also require an external server and custom application software to manage the zones.

Management of fabrics, like management of loop hubs, is normally provided over Ethernet, using SNMP or TELNET. Fabric switches may also be managed through the Fibre Channel link, using SES queries. Most fabric management applications are device managers; that is, they manage the switch enclosure but have no visibility to the rest of the SAN. If the switch vendor also manufactures loop hubs, an umbrella management platform that manages both fabric and loop hubs in the interconnect is viable. For enterprise networks, every new device manager implies an additional management console, and reducing this number via integrated SAN management is always desirable. Fabric management graphical interfaces may include topology mapping, enclosure and port statistics, and routing information and port performance graphing. These features give IT managers a snapshot of the fabric's status and throughput. The tendency of enterprise management for the LAN and WAN is to incorporate network snapshots into trending applications, such as Concord Network Health, which can be used for capacity planning and network analysis. As this trend extends to SANs, the SNMP data from fabrics can be queried to provide proactive information for storage network planning.

5.8 Fibre Channel–to–SCSI Bridges

When a new technology encroaches on an older one, transitional products can bridge the gap. Fibre Channel–to–SCSI bridges perform this function for the SAN by allowing legacy SCSI devices to participate in storage networking. Fibre Channel–to–SCSI bridges normally provide one or two Fibre Channel interfaces for SAN attachment and two to four SCSI ports for SCSI disk arrays or tape-backup subsystems. In addition to this physical and transport conversion, the Fibre Channel–to–SCSI bridge translates serial SCSI-3 protocol to the appropriate SCSI protocol required by the legacy devices.

The most common application for Fibre Channel–to–SCSI bridges is to support legacy tape-backup subsystems, as illustrated in Figure 5-11. Tape-backup and library systems represent a substantial investment and are not easily reengineered to support Fibre Channel. Tape backup, however, is an integral requirement for any storage network. Without a means to access a tape subsystem across Fibre Channel, less efficient means, such as backing up across the LAN, might be required. Fibre Channel–to–SCSI bridges therefore satisfy both the preservation of tape-subsystem hardware investment and the need to optimize the tape-backup process itself.

Placing a tape subsystem behind a Fibre Channel–to–SCSI bridge also removes ownership of the subsystem from an individual server. Since the tape subsystem is now addressable by any server on the storage network, all servers can share what was previously a dedicated

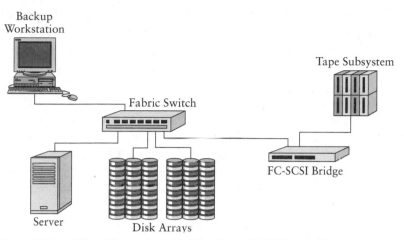

Figure 5-11 *A Fibre Channel–to–SCSI bridge with SCSI tape library*

resource. The separation of a tape subsystem from server ownership is taken a step further by other products discussed later.

The role of Fibre Channel–to–SCSI bridges will decline as legacy devices are eventually replaced by SAN-enabled systems. Given the large population and investment in traditional SCSI tape and disk products in use, however, Fibre Channel–to–SCSI bridges will continue to be useful options for SAN design for some time to come.

5.9 SAN Software Products

In addition to Fibre Channel storage and interconnect products, networking behind the server has led to the development of new software applications that leverage the potential of the SAN. Since storage networking itself was driven into existence by software applications—video, data mining, OLTP, and so on—the emergence of new applications continues the symbiotic cycle of hardware and software evolution. Server-clustering software, LAN-free and server-free backup utilities, file and volume management, and umbrella SAN management applications offer additional tools for building efficient, highly available storage networks. Server-clustering and tape-backup applications are discussed later; storage and SAN management applications are covered in more detail in Chapter 7.

Server clustering involves several aspects, including failover, load sharing, and common data access. As long as each server is tied to its own storage via parallel SCSI cabling, combining the resources of multiple servers efficiently is not possible. Separating servers from storage and then reconnecting them on a high-speed network topology enables storage to be accessed independently. This, in turn, facilitates deployment of storage for data-centric applications and eliminates access constraints of the server-centric model. If any server can provide a route to the same data, no server is indispensable. Fibre Channel thus enables server clustering, and server clustering enables a level of high availability assumed by enterprise networks that are moving applications from mainframes to UNIX and NT servers.

Failover for clustered servers may scale from 2 to more than 30 servers in a single configuration. Failover strategies are vendor-specific but generally require mutual monitoring of server status via a heartbeat protocol across a LAN interface (see Figure 5-12). In some implementations, a failover algorithm may trigger on the loss of an individual application or discrete server component, such as failure of a host bus adapter or LAN interface. The failure of an individual server's application or hardware element will be assumed by other servers in the cluster. If multiple servers are running the same application, additional middleware is required to ensure that servers do not overwrite shared data.

Coordinating the activity of multiple servers and safeguarding file access is no trivial task, which is reflected in the cost of clustering solutions. Compared to the cost of lost business due to down time, however, high availability via clustering is easily justified for mission-critical networks.

Tape backup is a universal requirement—and a universal problem—for all data networks, regardless of the specific topology used. Data security via backup is not only desirable but also is sometimes mandated by law. For server/storage configurations based on parallel SCSI, tape-backup strategies may require a dedicated tape-backup subsystem for each server, which optimizes performance but increases costs, or a centralized tape-backup configuration that requires a data path across the LAN, which reduces cost but hinders performance. As applications create ever-growing storage requirements, the time required to back up data increases. This backup window cannot be

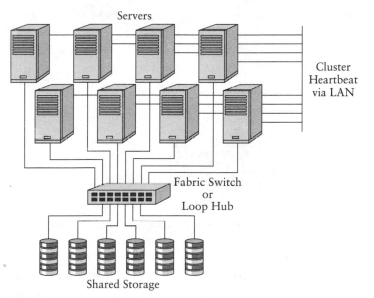

Figure 5-12 *SAN server clustering in eight-server configuration*

accommodated via the production or messaging LAN without intruding on user traffic. And, given the amount of data supported by an individual server, provisioning tape subsystems for every large server is cost-prohibitive.

Storage area networking is the only topology that facilitates an efficient centralization of tape backup that meets both cost and performance requirements. The first branch in the tape decision tree is the recognition that a separate network is required. LAN-free tape backup could, theoretically, be realized with a separate LAN, that is, dual-provisioning each server with Fast or Gigabit Ethernet cards to create a separate subnet for a tape-backup LAN. A storage network, however, provides a better solution, since both tape and other storage traffic can be concentrated on the same infrastructure and use native storage (SCSI) protocols.

Once the decision is made to build a separate topology to support tape requirements, other options are available. If tape-backup traffic can be segregated from the production LAN, can the overhead of tape backup be removed from the server? This becomes possible when

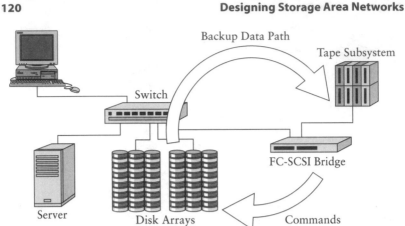

Figure 5-13 *LAN-free, server-free tape backup via TPC or NDMP*

servers are detached from their direct and exclusive connection to storage. Server-free backup is predicated on additional agents in the storage network; using backup-specific protocols, those agents can move data from autonomous, SAN-attached disks to autonomous, SAN-attached tape subsystems. Those agents may reside in dedicated servers, Fibre Channel switches, or Fibre Channel–to–SCSI bridges. The agent is responsible for accepting and executing scheduled backups, and the data path flows from the disk arrays to the agent and then to the tape subsystem, as shown in Figure 5-13. This removes the server from the tape-backup process, freeing its resources for user requests.

Two protocols have been formulated for server-free backup. Third Party Copy uses SCSI protocol extensions to bypass the server. Network Data Management Protocol (NDMP) provides a similar function but incorporates mechanisms for more granular features, such as backup of open files and permissions handling. Both approaches allow data backup to be performed without consuming server cycles and, due to the infrastructure provided by a SAN, without burdening the messaging network. An application study in Chapter 8 examines the migration from traditional backup to LAN-free and server-free backup in more detail.

5.10 Summary

GBICs

- GBICs are a critical component of the Fibre Channel transport.

- Vertical Cavity Surface Emitting Laser (VCSEL) GBICs provide higher reliability for fibre channel applications.

- Serial ID support allows GBICs to provide inventory and diagnostic status but requires management software for reporting.

Host Bus Adapters

- HBAs provide the interface between the host computer's bus architecture and the Fibre Channel network.

- HBA hardware, firmware, and device drivers fulfill Fibre Channel physical, link-level, framing, and upper-protocol requirements.

- For storage applications, the HBA maps Fibre Channel addressing to the SCSI bus/target/LUN identifier required by the operating system.

Fibre Channel RAID

- RAID is both a method for data distribution among multiple disks and a hardware implementation for disk arrays.

- RAID levels represent different techniques for improving performance and providing data security.

- Striping of data across multiple disks improves performance; mirroring of data provides redundancy. Parity algorithms may also be used to maximize speed and data integrity.

- Software RAID is performed by the host system; hardware RAID is normally performed by a controller within the disk array enclosure.

- A hardware RAID device may use parallel SCSI or Fibre Channel to interface between the disks and the RAID controller.

Fibre Channel JBODs

- JBODs (just a bunch of disks) are an economical means to provide Fibre Channel–attached storage.

- JBODs appear as loop segments and may be configured as single or redundant loops to disks.

- Disks within a JBOD may be addressed individually or assigned as sets for software RAID by a server.

- The overhead of software RAID across Fibre Channel may affect overall performance.

Arbitrated Loop Hubs

- Loop hubs facilitate wiring configurations and enable hot-insertion and removal of devices.

- Port-bypass circuitry and status indicators simplify network changes and elementary diagnostics.

- Repeater-based hubs provide better performance but must be engineered for jitter suppression.

- Retimer-based hubs eliminate jitter accumulation but incur performance overhead.

- Unmanaged hubs are economical but cannot provide protection against protocol-level events.

- Managed hubs may include loop integrity features based on protocol recognition circuitry.

Switching Hubs

- Switching hubs are based on a hybrid architecture that combines switched bandwidth with support for private loop devices.

- Switching hubs may allow multiple concurrent conversations on a single virtual loop.

Fabric Switches

- Fabric switches provide 100MBps per port and may support from 8 to 64 ports.

- Support for fabric port types (F_Port, FL_Port, E_Port) is vendor-specific.

- Port buffering allows frames to be queued and reduces frame discard under congested conditions.

- Fabric switches may also support private loop devices and port or address zoning.

- Management of fabric switches may be provided via SNMP, TELNET, SES, and other protocols.

Fibre Channel–to–SCSI Bridges

- Fibre Channel–to–SCSI bridges are transitional products that bring legacy SCSI disks and tape subsystems into the SAN.

- Fibre Channel–to–SCSI bridges allow tape subsystems to be shared by multiple servers.

Fibre Channel Software Products

- Server clustering software enables high-availability configurations on Fibre Channel.

- Storage management tape-backup software allows Fibre Channel–attached tape subsystems to be used by multiple servers and offloads backup from the LAN.

- Third Party Copy and Network Data Management Protocol (NDMP) software frees server resources by allowing direct disk-to-tape backup.

Problem Isolation in SANs

No network is bullet-proof. Even with careful selection of network equipment, cabling, and management applications, eventually something *will* break. The challenge, then, is to minimize the down time caused by a failure and to keep the rest of the network operational. In Fibre Channel environments, the design of HBAs, Arbitrated Loop hubs, and fabric switches, as well as SES controllers in JBODs and RAIDs, often includes features to detect and to isolate problems automatically and to provide alerts to management workstations. Autobypassing rogue ports, such as a port streaming LIP(F8)s, or raising an alert when a congestion threshold is reached enables the network operator to respond quickly to the error condition. Determining why the error occurred is facilitated if advanced diagnostic features are provided in the vendor's design. For more difficult problems, only a Fibre Channel analyzer is able to capture and decode frames completely and to furnish the level of detail necessary to diagnose a failure.

Error conditions may be classified in several categories, including physical layer, transport, framing, and upper-layer protocol (SCSI or IP). Physical-layer problems are most easily identified, since loss of a physical link will be reported via LEDs on an HBA, hub, or switch. A marginal GBIC or poor fiber-optic cabling, however, may still provide valid signal but corrupt the data stream and disrupt communication. Depending on the hub or fabric vendor's design, this condition may not be presented as an error. Products that integrate advanced diagnostic features prove their value when such failures occur, even if the advanced diagnostic utilities are not normally used in day-to-day network operations.

6.1 Simple Problem-Isolation Techniques

Generally, most error conditions are encountered during changes to a network's topology. This is particularly true during initial installation of the network, since new equipment is connected for the first time. In complex SAN installations, HBAs must be installed and their appropriate device drivers loaded, the cable plant laid, loop hubs and switches installed and configured, GBICs provisioned, and disk arrays properly deployed and cabled. Solutions providers typically preconfigure as many components as possible to simplify the installation process, but there is always an opportunity to cable devices together incorrectly or to omit steps in the installation procedure. Things happen.

Once the various SAN components have been configured, cabled, and powered on, operation is normally verified by a server's ability to access storage. If a server is unable to see part or all of the available disks, elementary troubleshooting begins. Depending on the server's operating system, it may simply be a matter of the SAN boot sequence. NT 4.0, for example, needs to have Fibre Channel disk arrays up and operational before its own device drivers load. Disks that are powered on after NT is booted may not be recognized by Disk Administrator, in which case NT itself must be reloaded to see the drives. This annoyance will, ideally, be resolved in a future release. The next logical step is to verify that the proper device drivers are installed for the Fibre Channel HBA. For preconfigured servers, this is assumed, and most HBA vendors provide utilities for driver installation and card diagnostics. Provisioning multiple HBAs in a single server requires attention to ensure that no resource conflicts occur and that each HBA is cabled to its appropriate hub or fabric switch.

Physical-layer problems can be diagnosed by verifying insertion or bypass status at the loop hub or fabric switch. Managed products facilitate this by replicating the physical LED status on a graphical interface and, depending on the vendor's implementation, by providing port-level diagnostics and status legends. For unmanaged hub products, LED states will at least indicate whether an attached device is providing valid Fibre Channel signal. Fabric switch LED status is typically more sophisticated, since in addition to valid Fibre Channel signal, the

LEDs may indicate whether an attached node has successfully logged on to the fabric.

Given a generic implementation of green and amber LEDs per port, as discussed in Chapter 5, the LED states can help determine the source of a physical-layer problem (see Table 6-1). Some states may not be valid for all products; for example, a loop hub with fixed copper ports will not display GBIC status.

Table 6-1   Port LED State Table

Green	Amber	Port State
Off	Off	No device attached
On	Off	Device attached and inserted
On	On	Device attached and bypassed
Off	On	Bad GBIC; port bypassed
Blinking	Blinking	Maintenance mode via management

Green Off/Amber Off: Normally, this would indicate that no device is installed on the port. For non-GBIC products, however, it may be possible to connect a cable, such as a DB-9 copper intracabinet cable, that carries no signal and consequently generates no port status. A GBIC-based product will recognize the presence of the GBIC and, depending on the status of the GBIC and signaling, light the appropriate LEDs.

Green On/Amber Off: The port is receiving valid Fibre Channel signal and has inserted the attached device. If communication is nonetheless disrupted, the cable lead from the port's transmit to the device's receiver may be broken. In Arbitrated Loop configurations, an HBA or array that sees nothing on its receiver will assume that the loop is down and will transmit a stream of LIP(F8) primitives. At the receiving end of that stream, the hub port will recover valid clock and will allow the device to insert. Without ordered-set recognition at the hub and policies to bypass a port streaming LIP(F8)s automatically, there will be no indication that a physical-cabling problem exists.

Troubleshooting this condition is difficult when copper cabling is used, since there is no immediate way to verify signal presence. For optical, non-OFC connections, disconnecting the cable at the HBA or the array allows visual verification of signal presence on the SC connector and thus speeds problem identification. Non-OFC laser is not harmful for short exposures, but it is always recommended to hold a small mirror or translucent paper over a fiber-optic connection before looking at the laser source. If no light is present on the fiber-optic SC connector, as shown in Figure 6-1, the likely cause is a break along the length of the cable lead. If light is present, lack of communication may be due to a number of other causes, including incorrect cable length or type, poor quality of cabling, dirty connectors, excessive jitter along the link, or protocol-level problems at the transport or upper layers. Using a known good cable in place of the existing run is usually the fastest means to verify the cable plant and to move on to the next branch in the troubleshooting decision tree.

Green On/Amber On: This state is a normal bypass condition. For unmanaged loop hubs, it indicates that a device is attached and, due to lack of valid Fibre Channel signal, has been bypassed. For managed loop hubs, it may indicate that bypass has occurred for another reason, such as excessive corruption of data at the protocol level or a streaming LIP(F8) condition. The hub's management workstation should provide specific information on the cause of the bypass. For fabric switches, it may indicate that a device is attached and has valid signal but has been unable to complete initialization or login to the fabric.

Since bypass mode may be triggered by loss of signal, disconnecting the cable at the hub or switch port allows verification of laser presence on the port's receive lead. Lack of laser light may indicate a break on the cable lead from the attached node's transmit running to the port's receiver. It may also indicate a problem with the node's transceiver, internal controller logic, or simply that the attached device is powered down. In mixed hub and fabric switch environments, lack of signal may also be caused by inadvertently connecting an OFC laser transceiver at the switch to a non-OFC transceiver at the hub.

Green Off/Amber On: This LED state reveals bad GBIC status, based on the port's reading of diagnostic pins on the GBIC connector. Verify that the GBIC is fully seated into the port, or move it to another port for status check before replacing.

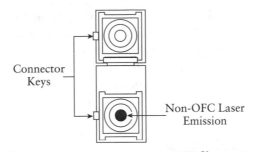

Figure 6-1 *Verifying signal presence on a non-OFC fiber-optic SC connector*

Diagnosing link-related problems is also facilitated by specialized diagnostic tools offered by several vendors. Hand-held analyzers for Fibre Channel cost less than $2,000 and provide link status for both transmit and receive leads, presence of valid Fibre Channel signal, presence of valid transmission words, and CRC error indicators. GBIC-based products offer more flexibility, since both copper and optical connections can be tested.

By logically troubleshooting from the link level through the upper transport and protocol layers, problem analysis can systematically eliminate potential sources and converge on problem identification. Signal presence and LED status can generally identify physical-layer issues, whereas protocol-related events require a higher intelligence in the hub. As discussed in Chapter 5, some managed loop hub, switching hub, and fabric switch products incorporate advanced diagnostic features. These range from proactive policies based on ordered set recognition to analyzerlike diagnostics that help pinpoint problems in the topology. Detecting frame CRC errors on a per port basis is useful, but identifying which AL_PA or port address generated the erred frame can tag the offending device more quickly. If the management graphical interface can display the protocol activity on all ports and has utilities for transmitting primitives to designated ports, the cycle of problem detection and recovery can be further shortened.

The trend toward integrated diagnostic functionality parallels the capabilities of some WAN/LAN router and ATM switch products, which include higher-level traffic capture and protocol decode facilities. The ability to crack frames and to provide protocol decode at

Fibre Channel speeds, however, would require significant buffering capability—over 100MB of memory for each second of traffic capture—and additional logic, which would make the interconnect price unreasonable. A full diagnostic of a SAN, therefore, requires a Fibre Channel analyzer and either in-house expertise or a contracted support organization with trained personnel to operate it.

6.2 Fibre Channel Analyzers

Fibre channel analyzers are to the SAN what Sniffers are to the WAN and LAN. A Sniffer on a Fast Ethernet segment (100Mbps) must capture a data stream at 10MBps to 12MBps, whereas a Fibre Channel analyzer must capture at ten times that rate. Fortunately, Fibre Channel analyzers do not cost ten times more than their WAN/LAN counterparts, but they are still expensive devices, costing $30,000 to $50,000, depending on features.

Fibre Channel analyzers intercept the gigabit data stream and eavesdrop on traffic. Through either manual control or preprogrammed triggers, the analyzer can capture several seconds, or several hundred megabytes, of activity at a time. Once the capture is performed, the analyzer decodes the data and displays the results, usually on an integrated monitor. Capture is typically run against one port at a time, although some vendor implementations allow data capture on two ports. The latter is particularly useful for capturing a transaction from both the initiator and the target perspectives.

In Arbitrated Loop topologies, the analyzer probes, such as GBICs, may be inserted into hub ports just upstream and downstream from a target port. This port-straddling configuration allows both in-bound and out-bound primitives and frames to be captured but is dependent on the availability of open hub ports. If adjacent ports are not available, other devices may have to be relocated on the hub to accommodate the probes. This may mask a physical-layer problem by altering the topology and components under examination. Alternatively, a device under investigation can be plugged directly into the analyzer, with the analyzer completing the circuit to the topology. The in-line configuration is mandatory for capturing fabric traffic, since there is no continuous path as in a loop. One drawback of the in-line method is that the connection between the node and the topology must be dis-

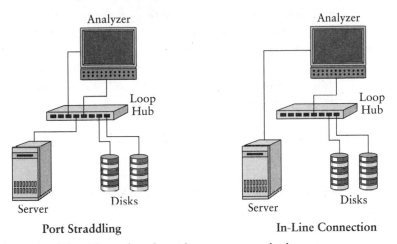

Figure 6.2 *Fibre Channel analyzer data-capture methods*

rupted to insert the analyzer. As with moving hub connections to accommodate straddling, the reconfiguration for in-line snooping may inadvertently mask problems. See Figure 6-2.

Triggering on a particular frame or protocol event, such as an ARB from a designated AL_PA, can be specified in a number of ways. Some analyzers offer utilities for composing complex trigger equations that allow capture to be executed on a series of conditions. The trigger event may mark the beginning of the trace or any assigned time frame within the capture window. Additionally, triggers may be defined to narrow the scope of the capture via start and end triggers.

The maximum amount of data that can be captured varies from vendor to vendor but generally does not exceed 2 seconds. Because IDLEs and other primitives may occur in series, the memory required to buffer captured data is reduced by simply counting the number of occurrences and logging those to the decode display. Thousands of consecutive IDLEs are thus collapsed into a single entry, which makes reading a trace much easier as well.

Once a capture is executed, the decode display will contain a sequential listing of all ordered-set and frame activity. Depending on the vendor's design, the trace will appear in one or more windows, with drill-down screens for detail of specific events. Trace field headers normally include a time stamp (to nanosecond granularity), a time delta from one event to the next, the analyzer port that saw the event, and ordered-set and frame information. (See Table 6-2.) Most Fibre Channel analyzers supply SCSI frame decode by default, with IP and other protocols as options. The drill-down for frame decode includes all frame fields, including routing control, source and destination IDs, frame controls, and data payload.

Table 6-2   Generic Fibre Channel Analyzer Fields

Time Stamp	Delta	Probe Port	Ordered Set	Frame Detail
000:00:10.887 502 600	.200	A	1 R_RDY	
000:00:10.887 502 600		A	13 ARB(F0)	
000:00:10.887 502 800	.200	B	12 IDLE	
000:00:10.887 503 200	.400	B	SOFi3	CMD READ

Analyzers may include, as integrated or accessory features, ordered-set and frame-generation capability, as well as the ability to induce protocol or frame errors for test purposes. Data generators are particularly useful for verifying proper operation of end devices, although this type of activity is normally conducted in a test lab environment. Vendors may also offer client/server versions of their products, to allow multiple diagnostic workstations to use a central analyzer resource.

In addition to diagnostic functions, analyzers provide performance statistics that can be used to monitor the impact of a particular application or configuration on the SAN. Since overloading a SAN segment can be one source of errors, port utilization data is very useful for understanding both link and upper-protocol issues. Some fabric switches and managed hubs also provide performance data. The combination of diagnostic features in loop hubs and fabrics with the detail provided by analyzers gives full visibility to the SAN and provides the toolset required to isolate and to recover from problems.

6.3 Summary

Simple Problem-Isolation Techniques

- Port-status LEDs on loop hubs and fabric switches can facilitate diagnosing elementary link-level problems.

- Presence of optical signaling may be verified at cable ends of both nodes and hub or switch ports.

- Loop hubs and switches may provide advanced diagnostics via a management interface for resolving protocol-related problems.

Fibre Channel Analyzers

- Fibre Channel analyzers are essential for troubleshooting to the frame level.

- Data capture is typically 1–2 seconds and may be triggered by specific protocol or frame conditions.

- Capture may be performed against one or two ports concurrently.

- Analyzers provide protocol decode and frame analysis utilities.

Management of SANs

Network management has one central objective: to maintain the stable transport of data across the network infrastructure. What is done with the data once it has arrived at its destination is normally outside the scope of traditional network management disciplines. As networking has emerged behind the server in the form of SANs, however, both the transport of data and the management of data are critical to stable operation. If two servers update the same file across a storage network, for example, data corruption can occur. And if the file's data is corrupted, the network's efficiency in transporting that data will not matter. Management of data resources, including file access, volume management, and data backup, is therefore as essential for SAN environments as is ensuring the reliable transport of data from one participant to another.

As long as the server/storage relationship was isolated from the network, storage management applications tended to be focused on the server—the direct owner of storage—and specific operating systems. Storage networking shifts the focus from the server to storage and enables storage management to address data issues apart from individual servers and independently of operating platform. With SANs, NT and UNIX servers are now able to share storage resources of a single RAID, and management of the RAID's resources may exist independently—for example, as a storage management entity—of either NT or UNIX environments. This abstraction from the previous server-centric model promises far more flexibility for resource allocation, volume management, and data security via backup.

As shown in Figure 7-1, management of the SAN is a hierarchy of functions that may exist as separate applications or as integrated management systems. Lower layers move status and event information up through the hierarchy, whereas upper layers issue commands and queries down to the appropriate agents below. The management structure is built on a foundation of managed devices that create the SAN interconnect—HBAs, loop hubs, switching hubs, Fibre Channel–to–SCSI bridges, and fabric switches—as well as SES (SCSI Enclosure Services) entities that may reside in disk arrays and tape subsystems. These devices communicate to their respective device management applications via a number of protocols, primarily Simple Network Management Protocol (SNMP) or SCSI Enclosure Services. The device management applications, in turn, may communicate to upper-level storage and storage resource managers, which may provide interfaces to enterprise-level systems management platforms. Fibre Channel hardware and software vendors have a vested interest in adapting their products to this umbrella management strategy, since cohesiveness of the various strata comprising SAN management facilitates deployment of all products.

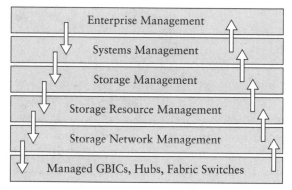

Figure 7-1 *Management hierarchy*

7.1 Storage Network Management

Storage network management is responsible for interfacing directly with interconnect equipment. The vendor of a managed network device supplies a console or a graphical interface that, at minimum, allows port configuration (insert/bypass) and reports basic enclosure status (power, fan, temperature). The feature set of a managed HBA, hub, or fabric switch is vendor-dependent. Some products offer only basic enclosure and port status, whereas others include utilization and diagnostic functions.

The application provided by the vendor to manage its product is a *device* manager, since typically the management scope does not extend beyond the product itself. A management utility for an HBA, for example, will give status, configuration, and port statistics for the HBA but will not provide visibility to hubs, fabric switches, or other nodes with which it communicates. The management of multiple storage network products implies multiple device managers and consequently, multiple management workstations or consoles to support various vendors' applications. Maintaining multiple management consoles is not an attractive option for IT administrators. Paralleling the evolution of network management in local and wide area networking, this fragmentation of management platforms provides incentives for consolidating device managers under one storage network application. Vendors that supply more pieces of the Fibre Channel interconnect may address consolidation by merging, for example, HBA, hub, and switch device managers into one management program, whereas vendors of point products, such as a fabric switch, may provide interfaces to third-party network management applications.

Device management has software, firmware, and hardware components (see Figure 7-2). Putting a loop hub port into bypass mode from a management console, for example, requires a management protocol, such as SNMP, to convey the command from the workstation to the loop hub. A management agent on-board the hub must then translate the bypass command into a hardware instruction, and the hardware, in turn, must raise or lower the appropriate leads to bypass the port physically.

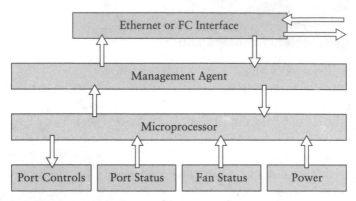

Figure 7-2 *Device management architecture*

The controller or firmware that supports the management agent is the Fibre Channel product's voice to the outside world. Communication between a device and its management workstation may be through the Fibre Channel transport using SES SCSI protocol, which is referred to as **in-band** management. Alternatively, management data may be segregated from Fibre Channel traffic via an external Ethernet, RS-232, or other interface, which is referred to as **out-of-band** management. Out-of-band management through Ethernet normally uses SNMP, although TELNET and Web browser implementations based on HTTP (HyperText Transfer Protocol) are also available. In-band and out-of-band solutions have their respective advantages and disadvantages, and some Fibre Channel products offer both to provide complementary functions. See Figure 7-3.

7.1.1 In-Band Management

Although it is possible to run SNMP/IP over Fibre Channel, the most prevalent in-band protocol for storage networks is SCSI Enclosure Services (SES). In order to support SES queries and commands, the Fibre Channel HBA, loop hub, or switch must contain an addressable Fibre Channel N_Port or NL_Port in the form of a Fibre Channel controller. The SES controller appears as an additional participant on the topology, which allows a Fibre Channel–attached management workstation to access it.

In-band management enables management functions that would be difficult to achieve via out-of-band methods. If a fabric switch, for

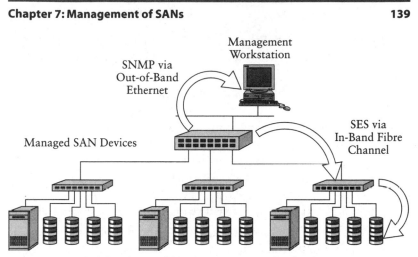

Figure 7-3 *In-band and out-of-band management data paths*

example, can initiate SES queries to its attached HBAs and disk arrays, it can provide a topology map of the SAN, detailing the identity, status, and port location of all SES-capable devices. In-band management also simplifies the storage network installation, since no additional LAN connections are required.

The significant drawback of any in-band management scheme is apparent when the Fibre Channel transport itself is down or disabled by excessive errors. Since all management data must move across the Fibre Channel network, loss of the transport means loss of management visibility to the managed devices and negates the ability to detect, isolate, and recover from network problems. Thus, although in-band management fulfills a useful function under stable network conditions, it is ill-equipped to deal with catastrophic physical-layer or transport-level events. In large, meshed fabrics, this vulnerability is obviated somewhat by providing redundant Fibre Channel links. Providing alternative Fibre Channel paths for management data, however, adds cost, consumes additional ports, and still does not eliminate the possibility that a management workstation will be rendered ineffectual if combinations of links or fabrics fail.

7.1.2 Out-of-Band Management

Out-of-band management avoids in-band issues by moving all management data off the production, or Fibre Channel, network. Out-of-band techniques typically use Ethernet for the management data path and wrap management queries or commands in SNMP, TELNET, or Web browser HTTP. Most Fibre Channel loop hubs and fabrics also provide a serial RS-232 console port as an alternative (but rarely used) access method.

Since out-of-band implementations do not rely on the Fibre Channel transport, management of loop hubs, fabrics, or Fibre Channel–to–SCSI bridges is still possible if the loop or fabric links are down. This is a significant advantage over in-band methods. Out-of-band management also facilitates integration of storage network management with enterprise management platforms, particularly those based on SNMP. The major weakness of out-of-band network management in Fibre Channel environments is its inability to provide autotopology mapping and other functions that require in-band communication between devices.

The most commonly used out-of-band protocols are SNMP, HTTP, and TELNET, all of which run over IP. The use of IP to carry management instructions and responses allows storage network devices to be managed from anywhere in a routed IP network. Storage network management can thus be colocated with the SAN or centralized with other IP-based network management applications in an enterprise network operating center (NOC).

7.1.3 SNMP

Simple Network Management Protocol (SNMP) is the predominant protocol for multivendor enterprise networks and is widely supported by routers and switches in wide and local area networking. SNMP provides a command set for soliciting status (SNMP Gets) or setting operational parameters (SNMP Sets) of target devices. An enterprisewide SNMP management platform is typically run as a graphical interface on a large UNIX or NT workstation and may poll hundreds of devices throughout the routed network. The management platform contains the SNMP manager; the managed router, hub, or switch contains an SNMP agent.

Device status information may include a variety of data points: serial number, vendor ID, enclosure status, port type, port operational state, traffic volumes, error conditions, and so on. This information is organized in a Management Information Base (MIB), which is maintained by both the management workstation and the SNMP agent within the managed device. For LAN and WAN management, several standard MIBs have been sanctioned by the internetworking community through a series of Requests for Comments (RFCs). If a vendor wishes to include additional device information that is not specified in a standard MIB, vendor-specific parameters or status can be compiled in a proprietary enterprise MIB, or MIB extension. Specific MIBs for Fibre Channel SANs have been under construction for some time and will, when adopted, allow multivendor storage networks to be managed with a common set of queries and commands.

Device information, status, and control variables within a MIB are organized in a hierarchical data structure, the Structure of Management Information (SMI). SMI defines an information tree whose branches lead to various management information bases and whose leaves are discrete data about a device's functionality and status. SMI notation, which is carried within an SNMP query or command, is essentially an address pointing to the location of the data requested by the management workstation.

In the MIB example given in Figure 7-4, the SMI notation 1.3.6.1.4.1.2490.1.1 points along multiple branches of the management tree and terminates at a vendor's MIB extension for Fibre Channel hub variables. Below this point, additional branches may lead to specific port, environment, and diagnostic values. With the adoption of standard Fibre Channel MIBs, common features shared by all vendors will migrate to standard MIBs, whereas vendor-specific functionality will remain in proprietary MIB extensions. This structure accommodates further feature enhancements without restricting vendors to the lowest-common-denominator management capability.

While providing the ability to query actively a device for status, SNMP also allows a device to generate a **trap,** or unsolicited status information. If a preconfigured error condition or threshold is reached, the managed device will initiate an SNMP message to the management workstation as an alert. On the management platform, the icon representing the managed device typically turns yellow or red, and the application may send a page or e-mail to the network operator. Because SNMP is a protocol shared by both the vendor's device management application and third-party management platforms, SNMP traps may be directed to either one. Integration into HP OpenView, for example,

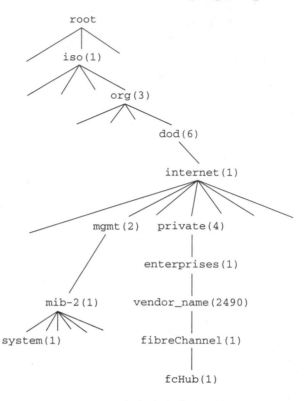

1.3.6.1.4.1.2490.1.1

Figure 7-4 *SNMP SMI notation for a vendor's loop hub values*

would allow a trap to be addressed to the OpenView management workstation, which could then automatically launch the vendor's device manager for further status or diagnosis of the problem.

Any management facility based on IP implies additional traffic on the messaging network. Although polling for all status information from multiple SNMP agents may generate noticeable overhead, SNMP management applications can reduce IP traffic by relying on traps for notification of events or by polling only for changes from an original status check. SNMP overhead is less of a concern in LANs based on switched Ethernet and WANs based on higher-speed Frame Relay or ATM links.

7.1.4 HTTP

Use of HyperText Transfer Protocol (HTTP) is a relatively new management tool that leverages the proliferation of Web browsers for managing network products. An HTTP management implementation has two components: an HTTP server that resides in firmware in the managed device and a Web browser, such as Netscape Navigator or Microsoft Explorer, that acts as a management graphical interface. By pointing the browser to the IP address of the managed device, the user can navigate a series of screens to monitor device status or to change device parameters.

Embedded HTTP capability is an entry-level management scheme and does not integrate into broader management applications as easily as SNMP or SES. Since a browser can be addressed to only a single IP target at a time, multiple instances of a browser application would have to be opened to manage multiple HTTP-based devices. Embedded HTTP management does not facilitate a comprehensive view of all managed products. Management-by-browser is therefore more suited for small SAN installations with a single loop hub or fabric to monitor. Recognizing that HTTP-based management has an appeal for the low end of the market, vendors of Fibre Channel products may provide both HTTP and SNMP management options.

Even with password protection at the managed device, HTTP presents a higher security risk than do other methods. All that is required to access an HTTP-managed loop hub or fabric is a browser, which everyone has, and the proper IP address, which can be hacked. At minimum, password protection should be provided for both read-only and read-write access, complemented by a firewall to prohibit external penetration of the customer network.

Browser-based management may also be implemented in a client/server configuration, as shown in Figure 7-5. A management workstation communicates with devices, using SNMP, and concurrently provides an HTTP server interface to remote browser consoles. This allows multiple remote managers to view the storage network via browsers and overcomes the single-device limitation of embedded HTTP management. By assigning read-only and read-write permissions, management operations can be provided for monitoring and modification controls.

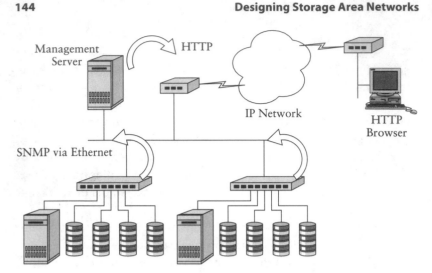

Figure 7-5 *Browser-based HTTP client/server management*

7.1.5 TELNET

Unlike typical SNMP or HTTP-based management solutions, a TEL-NET implementation is a text-only, command line interface. The user TELNETs across the IP network to the managed device—telnet 192.168.1.1—and establishes a session. The vendor, ideally, has provided one or two layers of password protection, beyond which a menu of commands is available. TELNET is normally used only to set the device's default IP address to one that can be used for SNMP access, but a command line interface alone is sometimes the tool of choice for UNIX environments.

The command set available and the status information that can be queried via TELNET is vendor-dependent. Some vendors offer only basic configuration commands, whereas others provide commands and queries for all functions that are available through the vendor's SNMP graphical interface.

7.1.6 Storage Network Management Issues

Storage network management faces several challenges previously encountered by local and wide area networking. In complex multivendor, multiplatform environments, customer requirements cannot be met with proprietary management solutions, even if a vendor offers a rich feature set for management of its own products. Open systems exert pressure on all vendors to seek common methods cooperatively while competing for market share with unique functionality. With both technical and political consequences, this contradiction slowly and sometimes painfully works its way through standards bodies and industry groups, although the net result of this process is always preferable to a closed, proprietary approach.

Since storage network management is shaped by the methods and capabilities of individual device managers, the configuration, status, and diagnostic features of each Fibre Channel network product are more useful if they are accessible through a common platform. Development of standard Fibre Channel MIBs, for example, simplifies the creation of comprehensive network management applications and enables higher-level storage management platforms to gather data from the SAN interconnect. From the customer's standpoint, the ability to manage a variety of products from a common interface has significant value because it consolidates network management consoles and streamlines staffing and training requirements.

A common application language also facilitates network management of the SAN. A single enterprise may have NT, Solaris, AIX, HP-UX, and other operating systems spread across the network. Network management may be centralized in an NOC or dispersed throughout individual business units. To accommodate the variety of platforms on which management applications may be run, the trend in Fibre Channel network management has been to port applications to a platform-independent language, such as Java. Adoption of Java has an additional benefit for customer deployment, since a single, multiplatform application reduces the number of software products and version levels that must be administered over time.

Status information from the underlying SAN components is another area that is critical to upper-level storage and systems management applications. Early implementations of device enclosure status (power/fan/temperature) and port state (enabled/bypassed) provided useful information for basic status but were incapable of supporting proactive management requirements. The ability to predict failures and to anticipate utilization trends requires more granular data points, including low-level CRC and transmission word error counters, bad ordered-set statistics, full GBIC status, per port frame transmit and receive statistics, and so on. As Fibre Channel HBA, hub, and fabric designs incorporate more detailed reporting, more useful information can be filtered and analyzed by upper-layer management applications.

7.2 Storage Resource Management

In the SAN management hierarchy, storage resource management (SRM) applications are a subset of more comprehensive storage management platforms. SRM applications are available as stand-alone programs or as plug-in modules for broader management applications and are written to either homogeneous or heterogeneous operating system environments. The primary value these programs offer is the ability to make all distributed disk assets visible to a single management console. Since SRM applications are focused exclusively on storage availability and utilization, how that storage is physically connected to servers is largely transparent. SRM applications are therefore not unique to SANs but may encompass internal workstation-attached, SCSI-attached, and NAS storage as well. The SAN-specific features of a storage resource application surface when, via the Fibre Channel topology, multiple servers have access to the same storage arrays and when the SRM workstation itself is SAN-attached.

Without a storage resource mechanism, disk administration is limited to individual servers. For an enterprise with hundreds or thousands of servers and, consequently, hundreds or thousands of disks and arrays, manually consolidating information on disk utilization, location of operating systems, location of common applications, the amount of disk space budgeted for users or departments, and so on, is overwhelming. As a consequence, applications are unnecessarily duplicated on multiple servers, disk space is underutilized in some departments and overutilized in others, tape-backup requirements cannot be properly sized, and sudden outages due to disk starvation cannot be anticipated.

Storage resource management addresses these shortcomings by automating the process of disk information retrieval and presenting a single view of all disk resources. SRM client software on each server periodically updates information on its assigned volumes and directories and forwards this data to the SRM manager. The SRM management platform, in turn, consolidates the status information from multiple clients in a relational database and may, depending on the vendor's implementation, provide storage policies that issue alerts when usage thresholds are exceeded. Similar to trending tools in local and wide area networks, SRM applications may also offer enhanced capacity-planning utilities that facilitate redistribution of storage resources and provide data for accurate budget forecasts of impending storage needs.

Because SANs enable a storage-centric model, SRM applications can be leveraged more effectively for optimal use of storage than can fixed SCSI configurations. JBODs and RAIDs on a storage network, for example, offer more flexibility in redistribution of disk space between SAN-attached servers and more easily accommodate increasing the pool of storage without system down time. At a higher level, storage utilization data via SRM can be correlated with transport utilization via storage network management to determine the optimum configuration of servers and storage to meet capacity requirements and traffic patterns.

7.3 Storage Management

Storage management—also referred to as enterprise storage management—is a broader category of storage functions that may, in addition to asset tracking, include tape backup, archive, data placement, and volume and file policy administration. A storage management application may be an umbrella, multifunction platform, packaged as a suite of complementary software products or as stand-alone programs dedicated to specific management functions, such as tape backup. Like SRM applications, storage management is facilitated by, but not dependent on, storage area network topologies. Vendors of storage management products, however, have become SAN proponents, due largely to the greater flexibility that SANs provide over other storage configurations.

As discussed in Chapter 5, tape backup is a universal requirement for storage applications and a universal problem as the amount of distributed storage to be backed up increases. Fibre Channel enables LAN-free and server-free backup strategies by providing a dedicated storage network on which servers, storage, tape, and intelligent backup agents may reside. Assigning which tape subsystems on the SAN are responsible for individual RAIDs and arrays, how often backups of some systems should occur, sizing the backup window to the amount of data to be backed up, performing restore operations when required, and scheduling backups for optimal performance are all tasks of the storage management application.

In addition to backup operations, storage management functions may monitor access to shared resources, such as tape libraries or optical archives; schedule nondisruptive disk defragmentation routines; manage the growth and integrity of file systems; and oversee cross-platform access to storage. The more tightly integrated these activities are within a single application, the simpler storage administration becomes for day-to-day operations. As more storage, tape, and archive systems appear on the SAN, integration is further enhanced, since the storage management platform itself can access resources directly without having to pass through servers.

7.4 Storage, Systems, and Enterprise Management Integration

Systems management applications consolidate the process of monitoring and controlling network resources and often encompass under a single application umbrella various networks within an enterprise. A systems management application may be dedicated to a specific function, such as utilization and performance of all network resources, or incorporate related categories across multiple networks, such as asset and accounting control for tracking resources and billing individual departments' usage of network equipment and bandwidth. Systems management functions, such as security management and fault management, span wide area, local area, and storage networks and so require common interfaces to all topologies.

Enterprise management applications embrace all or most of the individual systems disciplines and provide the most comprehensive view of all corporate network resources. Sitting at the top of the management food chain, enterprise management relies on a steady diet of status, statistics, configuration, utilization, performance, and other management data fed by the underlying management subsystems and entities. Since storage networking introduces another rich set of data points for systems and enterprise management, initiatives have been proposed to rationalize the flow of management data between the lowest-level network structures and the upper-level, enterprisewide management applications.

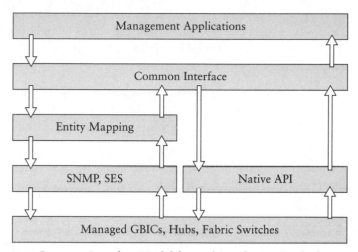

Figure 7-6 *Common Interface Model for multivendor, cross-platform management*

For storage networking, the first step in this process is to integrate the storage-specific functions of management through a common interface model or API (application programming interface). (See Figure 7-6). Current initiatives for this integration include Microsoft's Common Information Model (CIM) for more global network management and Sun Microsystems' StoreX project for storage management. By providing a common set of commands and status definitions for all storage and storage networking products, upper-level applications can be written without the overhead of porting to individual products or protocols. The Storage Networking Industry Association (SNIA) has created a number of work groups to address storage management integration, which will, in turn, facilitate integration to upper-level systems and enterprise applications.

7.5 Summary

Storage Network Management

- Management of SANs falls within a hierarchy of management applications, extending from hardware device managers through enterprisewide management applications.

- Device managers convey commands and status from hardware to an external management application, typically via SNMP, HTTP, or SES.

- Storage network management relies on information from device managers and consolidates management data into a comprehensive view of the SAN interconnect.

- In-band management moves management data across the Fibre Channel transport. Out-of-band management relies on SNMP, HTTP, or other protocols to move SAN management data via Ethernet.

- Standardization of Fibre Channel MIBs facilitates multivendor network management applications.

Storage Resource Management

- Storage resource management provides a consolidated view of distributed disk resources, available space, file locations, user storage budgets, and so on, and facilitates capacity planning.

Storage Management

- Storage management may include resource functions and adds tape-backup management, data archiving, data placement, and file policy administration.

- Storage management applications are facilitated by the SAN's ability to share tape and storage resources.

Storage, Systems, and Enterprise Management Integration

- Management of storage and storage networking may be integrated into higher-level systems and enterprise management applications.

- Integration is facilitated by common programming interfaces.

Application Studies

Although SANs share common components in the form of servers, storage, and interconnect devices, the configuration of a storage network is determined by the application problems it resolves. The requirements for a full-motion video application differ from those for high-availability OLTP (online transaction processing). LAN-free tape-backup applications may use unique hardware and software products that would not appear in a SAN designed around server-clustering requirements. Because SANs offer the flexibility of networking, however, it is possible to satisfy the needs of multiple applications within a single networked configuration, just as a LAN backbone may service disparate applications for an enterprise.

The following application studies examine SAN installations that were designed to meet specific requirements. In some instances, the deployment of a new networked infrastructure has provided additional opportunities for resolving unrelated issues. A SAN designed for a high-bandwidth application, for example, also facilitates a more efficient tape-backup solution. Although SANs are not a panacea for every storage application need, the building blocks that SANs provide can be used to construct a wide range of viable solutions unattainable by other means.

8.1 Full-Motion Video

Using one of the first applications of Fibre Channel technology, full-motion video editing and broadcast companies have leveraged the bandwidth, distance, and shared resources that SANs enable. Digitized video has several unique requirements, including the sustained transmission of multiple 30MBps streams and intolerance for disruption or delays, that exceed the capabilities of legacy data transports. Most SAN-based video applications use the SCSI-3 protocol to move data from disk to workstations, although custom configurations have been engineered using IP for multicast and broadcast distribution.

Some of the first video SANs used Arbitrated Loop for the underlying topology. An efficiently designed loop will support three video streams but is susceptible to the potential disruption of LIPs or loss of all streams if a node on the shared transport misbehaves. The dedicated bandwidth that a fabric provides is more suitable for video applications but requires fabric services that were not originally available for HBAs and disks. A number of installations in use today are therefore based on private loop switching. Loop switching accommodates the various levels of private loop HBAs in workstations (NT, Mac, SGI, and so on) while offering the connectivity and per port throughput of a fabric switch. As HBA and disk vendors have developed fabric service support on their products, fabrics have gradually displaced loop switching for these operations.

Video applications have common transport requirements but vary considerably in content. A video-editing application may center on a workgroup configuration, as shown in Figure 8-1, allowing peer workstations to access and to modify video streams from one or more disk arrays. In addition to the physical SAN topology, any application that allows data sharing must have software support for file access and locking by multiple users. A video broadcast application that serves up content from a central data source to multiple feeds must have the means to support IP multicast across the Fibre Channel network. Video used for training applications may support both editing workstations and user stations, with random access to shared video clips or instructional modules digitized on disk.

Video over Fibre Channel has appeared in some surprising locations, such as on the desktops of football coaches for major university and professional teams. Although it has been common practice to use video tapes of major games to analyze player performance and the strategy of the opposing teams, the mechanical limitations of video tape make it difficult to access individual plays quickly for analysis. Access to archived games is also difficult, since tapes must be cata-

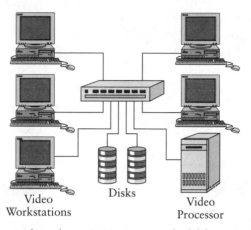

Video Workstations

Disks

Video Processor

Figure 8-1 *A peer video-editing SAN via a switched fabric*

loged, stored, and manually mounted for playback. These limitations are overcome by digitizing video to disk via editing workstations and then marking the play sequences with software pointers. A coach can then pull up any desired portion of a game for playback, using recorder-type controls for slow motion, rewind, and stop motion. The storage requirements for such an application are quite high—potentially terabytes of data—as is the bandwidth required to drive multiple coach workstations and training rooms for players. Distance is also a factor, since workstations may be spread across an entire floor or multiple floors of a facility.

Figure 8-2 depicts a small SAN configuration for shared access to digitized video stored on disk. Since the retrieved plays are relatively short and are called up at random, the duration of video streaming to multiple coach stations is sporadic, bursty traffic. This prevents the 100MBps cascade link between the storage/editing switch and the coach/training switch from becoming a bottleneck, as it might if the streams were persistent. The video-editing workstations are used to load the digitized video to disk and to place software markers for plays and so are best positioned on the same fabric as the disk arrays. This simple configuration is expanded to support additional coach stations by cascading more fabric switches from the root, storage/editing switch. Some installations of this type may have 20 or more coach stations interconnected by the SAN.

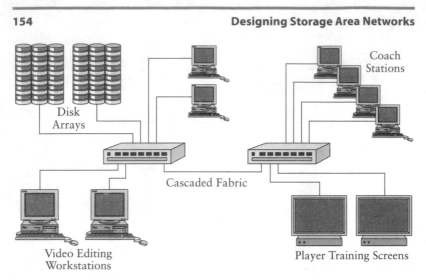

Figure 8-2 *Video SAN for sports training*

Although the Fibre Channel fabric switches, HBAs, and disk arrays enable this application to be implemented, the SAN-specific components are the least expensive items in the configuration. The software required to convert and to catalog the digitized data and to create a user interface that facilitates play analysis represents the major portion of the investment. According to the coaches who use these systems, the return on investment is amply demonstrated by the games they have won.

8.2 Prepress Operations

Prepress refers to the creation and modification of graphical images for advertisements, catalogs, and posters. Graphics can be as simple as low-resolution black-and-white newspaper ads or as sophisticated as large, four-color, high-resolution images that are applied to billboards or city buses.

Unlike full-motion video applications, computerized prepress data traffic is always bursty in nature. A single graphics image is read from disk, rendered for several hours by a graphics artist at a workstation, and written back to disk. The file may pass through multiple revisions, and therefore multiple workstations, as other detail, titles, and legends are added. When graphical editing is complete, the file is then read by a preprint processor for conversion from digital format to hardcopy or print negative.

Since a graphical image must go through a series of editing steps, each by a different artist, as it passes through the production process, file ownership is critical for maintaining data integrity. If the same image is inadvertently opened and modified at the same time, hours of work can be lost. Software companies that specialize in prepress operations resolve this potential problem by providing file-sharing middleware. This software resides on each workstation and, by intercepting calls from the operating system to the file system, allows file ownership to be transferred serially from one user to another as the file is read from and written back to disk.

In addition to file ownership, the amount of time it takes to read a large graphics image from disk for editing and to write back the modified version is an important issue for prepress. Read/write time is, for the user, down time, and the accumulated down time between edits can impact the entire production process. For larger prepress operations in particular, the bandwidth supplied by a LAN is insufficient for concurrent file transfers of image files that are often in the hundreds of megabytes.

Like video applications, prepress has a voracious appetite for storage. A catalog production, for example, may require hundreds of gigabytes of storage for high-resolution photographic images and formatting information. A major brands consumer catalog may have three or more editions per year, with revisions of some product images and introduction of new ones. All of this data must be maintained and accessible for updates. File compression helps reduce the overall storage requirement but is less effective for high-resolution images.

SANs were introduced into prepress operations primarily by vendors of file-access software. As a total solution, the combination of file-access middleware, higher bandwidth and shared storage via Fibre Channel, and increased storage capacity provided by Fibre Channel disk arrays addresses most of the data infrastructure issues prepress operators face.

In Figure 8-3, graphics artists are segmented into smaller, shared 100MBps loops, whereas RAID disk enclosures reside on dedicated 100MBps links via a fabric switch. The distribution of users is scalable, since additional users may be accommodated with other loop segments

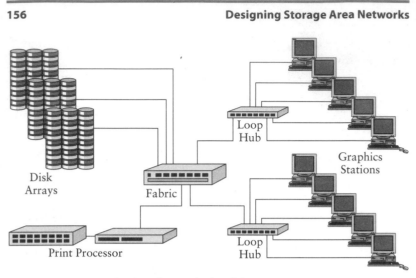

Figure 8-3 *Prepress SAN with switched and loop segments*

and the population of each loop adjusted according to workload and bandwidth requirements. Shared storage in this configuration is also scalable, both by the addition of drives into the RAID enclosures and by attachment of new arrays over time. Specialized preprint processors are brought into the SAN via Fibre Channel–to–SCSI bridges. And finally, file-access software on each graphics workstation ensures that a file can be modified by only one user at a time and that the identity of the current owner is known. This SAN solution also provides greater efficiency by transporting graphics files with SCSI protocol, as opposed to IP or IPX overhead required by a LAN transport.

8.3 LAN-Free and Server-Free Tape Backup

For IT operations, tape backup poses a number of problems, none of which is easily addressed by traditional parallel SCSI or LAN-based methods. As long as disk arrays are bound to individual servers, tape-backup options are limited to server-attached tape subsystems or transport of backup data across the messaging network. Provisioning each server with its own tape-backup system is an expensive solution and requires additional overhead for administration of scheduling and tape rotation on multiple tape units. Performing backups across the production LAN allows for the centralization of administration to one or

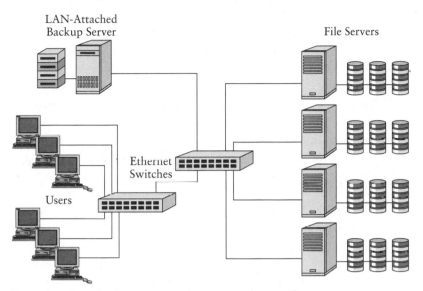

Figure 8-4 *Tape backup across a departmental network*

more large tape subsystems but burdens the messaging network with much higher traffic volumes during backup operations. In addition, scheduling backups for multiple servers to a central tape resource creates an inherent contradiction between the time required to back up all servers and the time available for nondisruptive access to the network. Scheduling backups during nonpeak hours—8:00 P.M. to 6:00 A.M.— may not provide sufficient time to back up all data and is not an option for enterprises that operate across multiple or international time zones.

In Figure 8-4, four departmental servers share a common tape-backup resource across the production LAN. Even with switched 100Mbps Ethernet and no competing user traffic, the maximum sustained throughput from server to tape is approximately 25GB (gigabytes) per hour. If each server supports a very moderate 100GB of data, a full backup of the department's data would require 16 hours. Backups, however, are normally scheduled for incremental backup of changed files on a daily basis, with full disk backups occurring only once a month or quarter. To accommodate both full and incremental backups, the full-backup routines would have to be rotated among different servers on different days and then only during periods when full LAN bandwidth was available.

As the volume of data exceeds the allowable backup window and stresses the bandwidth capacity of the messaging network, either the bandwidth of the messaging network must be increased or the backup data must be removed from the messaging network altogether. Installing a high-speed LAN transport, such as switched Gigabit Ethernet, can alleviate the burden on the production network but leaves the server/storage relationship unchanged. Just as the user saturation of 10Mbps Ethernet engendered 100Mbps Ethernet and the saturation of 100Mbps Ethernet begot Gigabit Ethernet, opening larger pipes on the LAN may not provide a long-term solution. If you build bandwidth, user data will come. Resolving the potential conflict between user traffic and storage-backup requirements is accomplished, therefore, only by isolating each onto separate networks. A storage network removes backup data from the production network, provides an equivalent high-speed transport to Gigabit Ethernet, and, by separating servers from storage, allows other backup and storage technologies to emerge.

As a transitional configuration, the SAN in Figure 8-5 is installed solely to offload the production network. Existing parallel SCSI-attached drives are left intact, and the new components include only Fibre Channel HBAs, a loop hub or fabric switch, and a Fibre Channel–to–SCSI bridge. Since the tape subsystem appears to each server as another SCSI device on a separate SCSI bus, it is accessible to the tape-backup client residing on each server. The backup scheduler instructs each server when and what kind of backup to perform on a sequential basis. Since the backup data path is now across a dedicated SAN, the constraints of the messaging network are removed from the backup process, and the burden of backup traffic is removed from the LAN.

The 100MBps bandwidth provided by Fibre Channel and the flexibility of moving backup data on its own transport, however, do not resolve every issue associated with this backup implementation. Although the SAN transport may allow backup data to move at high speed, other limiting factors include server performance, data rate of the parallel SCSI drives, the type of data being backed up, performance of the FC-SCSI bridge, and the throughput of the tape subsystem itself. The slowest component in a backup configuration is usually determined by the tape drive's sustained streaming rate. A tape unit may be able to stream only 10MBps to 15MBps and so cannot fully use the

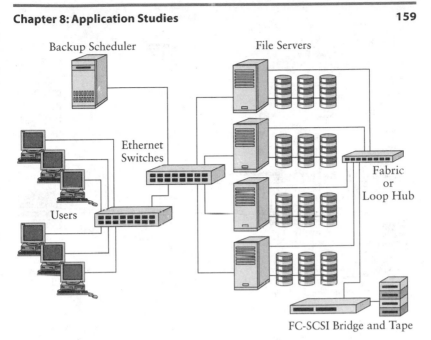

Figure 8-5 *Transitional LAN-free backup implementation*

bandwidth Fibre Channel makes available. The overall time required for full backups is thus improved only moderately by Fibre Channel, although the scheduling itself is no longer dependent on or interferes with LAN traffic patterns.

Since each of the four servers is now provisioned with a Fibre Channel HBA, other options are available for reducing backup times. Some Fibre Channel–to–SCSI bridges offer two Fibre Channel interfaces. If the SAN interconnect is a fabric switch, two servers can perform concurrent backups to two bridge-attached tape subsystems, thus cutting the overall backup time in half.

Optimizing the backup routine further requires several additional SAN components. Moving disk storage from parallel SCSI to Fibre Channel–attached arrays offers, among other things, the ability to remove the server from the backup data path. This is the most significant improvement from the standpoint of performance and nondisruptive backup operations. If server resources are freed from backup tasks, the servers are always available for user access. And if the backup process itself does not interfere with user access to data, the

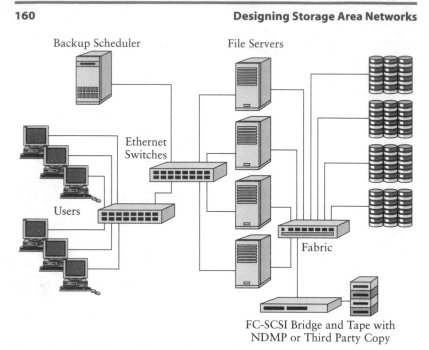

Figure 8-6 *LAN-free and server-free tape-backup installation*

backup window is no longer defined by users or the relatively slow performance of the tape subsystem.

Backups may be performed at any time, provided that the backup software handles file permissions and updates and that a Fibre Channel–attached backup agent exists to buffer data from disk to tape. The backup agent may exist as an NDMP (Network Data Management Protocol) or as a Third Party Copy protocol utility resident on the interconnect, a dedicated Fibre Channel–attached backup server, or in a Fibre Channel–to–SCSI bridge or native Fibre Channel tape subsystem.

Figure 8-6 demonstrates an extension of the departmental tape-backup solution that incorporates Fibre Channel–attached disk arrays and a Third Party Copy or NDMP utility resident on a Fibre Channel–to–SCSI bridge. In this configuration, backup data is read directly from disk by the copy agent and written to tape, bypassing the server. Whereas the SAN provides the vehicle to move the backup data, the backup software must control when and where to move it. Concurrent backup and user access to the same data are possible if the backup protocol maintains metadata—file information about the actual data—to track changes that users may make to data, such as records, as it is being written to tape. As higher-performance native Fibre Channel tape subsystems become available, the ability to back up and to restore over the SAN will better accommodate the growing volume of data that enterprises generate.

8.4 Server Clustering

As enterprise applications have shifted from mainframe and midrange systems to application and file servers, the reliable access to data that the legacy systems provided—and that required decades of engineering to accomplish—has been compromised. To make their products acceptable for enterprise use, server manufacturers have responded with more sophisticated designs that offer dual power supplies, dual LAN interfaces, multiple processors, and other features to enhance performance and availability. The potential failure of an individual component within a server is thus accommodated with redundancy. Redundancy typically implies hardware features but may also include redundant software components, including applications. Extending this strategy, redundancy may also be provided simply by duplicating the servers, with multiple servers running identical applications. The failure of a hardware or software module within a server is accommodated by shifting users from the failed server to one or more servers in a cluster.

The software required to reassign users from one server to another with minimal disruption to applications is very complex. Clustering software written for high-availability implementations may trigger on the failure of a component of the hardware, protocol, or application. The recovery process must preserve user network addressing, login information, current status, open applications, open files, and so on. This is no small task, which may in part account for the delays in embedding clustering into the operating system. Clustering software may also include the ability to load-balance between active servers, so that in addition to failover support, the servers in a cluster can be maximized for increasing overall performance.

Small clusters can be deployed with traditional parallel SCSI cabling for shared data but are generally limited to two servers. Fibre Channel allows server clusters to scale to very large shared data configurations, with more than a hundred servers in a single cluster. Whether this is implemented with Arbitrated Loop or a combination of fabrics and loop depends on the traffic volumes required by user applications.

Since the focus of clustering is to facilitate availability, deploying a server cluster on a SAN typically includes redundant paths from multiple servers to data. Software on each server must monitor the health of hardware components and applications and be able to inform other servers in the cluster if a failure or loss of service occurs. This heartbeat status is normally propagated over a dedicated, and sometimes redundant, LAN interface. If redundant paths to data are provided, each server must also monitor the status of each SAN connection and redirect storage traffic if a loop or switch segment fails. In addition, the data itself may be secured via local or remote RAID mirroring, which provides a duplicate copy if a primary storage unit fails. This tiered strategy helps ensure the availability of servers, access to data, and the data itself.

In the site represented in Figure 8-7, a cluster of ten servers is supported by Arbitrated Loop in a redundant, shared data scheme. Two 12-port loop hubs are configured as primary and backup paths between the clustered servers and RAID disk arrays. For this installation, the status heartbeat is also configured with redundant Ethernet links between each server, so that the failure of an Ethernet link will not falsely trigger a condition in which each server would attempt to assume services for others. Since the clustering software determines what components or applications on each server should be covered by a failure, subsets of recovery policies can be defined within the ten-server cluster. In this configuration, all servers share a common database application, whereas subsets of three servers are configured for failover for specific user applications. The example configuration can also be scaled to accommodate additional servers or storage by either cascading additional hubs on each loop or, depending on bandwidth requirements, subdividing primary and backup loops into smaller segments, using switching hubs or fabrics.

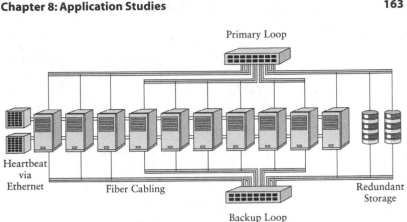

Figure 8-7 labels: Primary Loop, Heartbeat via Ethernet, Fiber Cabling, Backup Loop, Redundant Storage

Figure 8-7 *A fully redundant server cluster using Arbitrated Loop for shared access*

8.5 Internet Service Providers

Internet service providers, or ISPs, that provide Web hosting services have traditionally implemented servers with internal or SCSI-attached storage. For smaller ISPs, internal or direct attached disks are sufficient as long as storage requirements do not exceed the capacity of those devices. For larger ISPs hosting multiple sites, storage requirements may exceed SCSI-attached capacity of individual servers. Implementation of network-attached storage (NAS) or SANs are both viable options for supplying additional data storage for these configurations.

In addition to storage needs, maintaining availability of Web services is critical for ISP operations. Because access to a Web site—URL, or uniform resource locator—is based on Domain Name System (DNS) rather than physical addressing, it is possible to deploy redundant Web servers as a failover strategy. If a primary server fails, another server can assume access responsibility via a round-robin DNS address resolution. For sites that rely on internal or SCSI-attached storage, this implies that each server and its attached storage must maintain a duplicate copy of data. This is a workable solution so long as the data itself is not dynamic, that is, consists primarily of read-only information. It is a less attractive option, however, for e-commerce

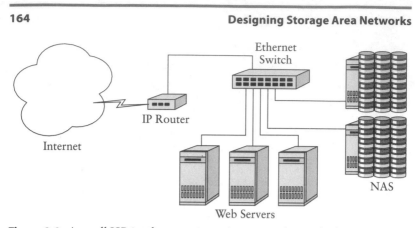

Figure 8-8 *A small ISP implementation using network-attached storage*

applications, which must continually update user data, on-line orders, and inventory tracking information. The shift from read-mostly to more dynamic read-write requirements encourages the separation of storage from individual servers. With NAS or SAN-attached disk arrays, data is more easily mirrored for redundancy and is made available to multiple servers for failover operation. As Figure 8-8 illustrates, NAS provides common data access over shared or switched Ethernet, allowing multiple Web servers to exist in a failover configuration.

SAN architecture brings additional benefits to ISP configurations by freeing up bandwidth on the provider's LAN segments, providing high-speed data access between servers and storage, and facilitating tape-backup operations. As shown in Figure 8-9, storage traffic is isolated from the LAN data path, which helps ensure data integrity even if problems occur on the LAN transport. At the same time, read-write operations to disk do not burden the LAN with additional traffic, which allows the LAN to be designed around external access requirements alone. LAN or server-free backup is enabled by SAN-attached tape subsystem and NDMP or Third Party Copy software utilities, which further frees LAN bandwidth for users. Expansion of storage and growth of Web servers are accommodated by extending the SAN with additional fabric switches or loop hubs. This small configuration can scale to hundreds of servers and terabytes of data, with no degradation of service.

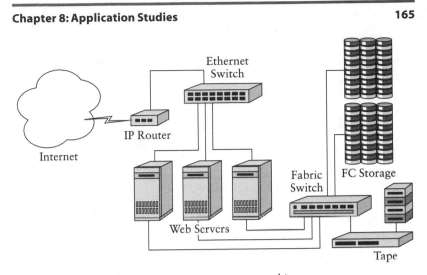

Figure 8-9 *ISP configuration using storage networking*

8.6 Campus Storage Networks

Server-based applications and storage present several contradictions for IT management of extended networks. Decentralized servers and storage provide the convenience and higher speed of local user access but require higher administrative overhead for maintaining and backing up multiple sites. Centralizing servers and storage to a data center reduces administrative requirements and allows consolidation of server resources but restricts remote users to the bandwidth available via the WAN. Traditionally, centralizing resources has meant provisioning multiple high-speed WAN links to each site just to achieve 1MBps to 5MBps bandwidth, which is often insufficient to supply the response time users demand. Even with high-performance routers and data-compression techniques, the WAN may become a bottleneck for both peer traffic and file retrieval between remote sites and a data center.

Fibre Channel's support of 10-km links facilitates the search for a compromise between distributed and centralized data access. Using longwave lasers and multimode cabling, multiple sites in a campus or metropolitan-area network can be brought together in an extended SAN. As shown in Figure 8-10, each building has a local SAN, which,

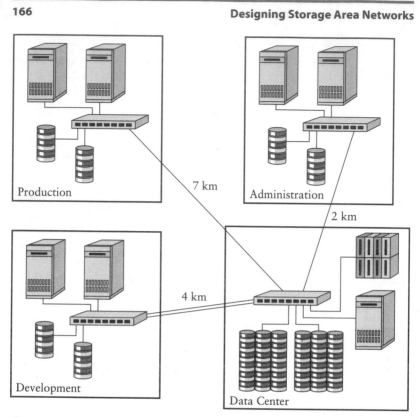

Figure 8-10 *Campus storage network*

depending on traffic requirements, is based on Arbitrated Loop or a departmental fabric switch. The local SAN provides high-speed access and storage sharing for the users at each site. By linking remote sites to a central data center via single-mode fiber, servers at each remote location also have access to centralized storage. This configuration also allows each remote site to be backed up to large tape subsystems maintained by the data center. In the example shown, the development building is provisioned with two fiber-optic links. This is to accommodate retrieval of engineering drawing files archived on data center RAIDs. By load-balancing across multiple switch links, an effective throughput of up to 200MBps can be achieved.

This extended SAN helps resolve data security issues via backup and sharing of centralized storage by multiple remote locations but still requires software to control volume assignment and file locking if data is to be shared among remote servers. Particularly in NT environments, it is essential to administer which storage devices an NT server can access. Common access to a shared tape subsystem likewise requires scheduling software and the ability to alter ownership of the tape resource dynamically, such as via zoning on a fabric switch.

8.7 Disaster Recovery

Similar to campus SANs, disaster-recovery implementations are leveraging Fibre Channel's support for 10-km 100MBps links to provide remote disk mirroring and tape-backup requirements. Using Fibre Channel extenders, it is possible to achieve distances of more than 60 km if the disaster-recovery site is more than 10 km away. Enterprise networks that invest in disaster-recovery will normally deploy additional safeguards, including high-availability server clustering, RAID, and redundant data paths via dual loops or fabric switches.

Figure 8-11 illustrates a disaster-recovery solution that uses long-wave, single-mode fiber cabling between the production and disaster-recovery sites, with fully redundant data paths for each location. To avoid propagation delays for every transaction, each site is configured with fabric switches instead of Arbitrated Loop hubs. This provides higher-speed access at the production site, with only disaster recovery–specific traffic traversing the long haul. In the example shown, the primary application at the production site is a relational database. To keep the disaster-recovery site current, only updated records are required, which further reduces the burden on the 6-mile link. Periodic tape backup can be performed against the disaster-recovery disks, which achieves the goal of data security without incurring additional

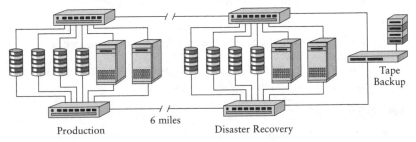

Figure 8-11 *Fibre Channel–based disaster-recovery implementation*

overhead on the production servers. Redundant data paths at each location prevent the failure of a link or a switch from disrupting either production or data-copying applications, whereas dual Fibre Channel connections to the Fibre Channel–to–SCSI bridge ensure that a path is always available for the tape subsystem. This configuration could be further optimized, at some expense, by deploying two fibers for each 6-mile link, thus increasing the capacity to 200MBps, if desired.

8.8 Summary

Full-Motion Video

- At ~30MBps per stream, Fibre Channel can support multiple sustained full-motion video streams on a single 100MBps pipe.

- The majority of SAN-based video applications use SCSI protocol, although IP implementations allow for multicast applications.

- Video streams are intolerant of interruptions and so are more suited to fabrics than to Arbitrated Loops.

Prepress Operations

- Prepress applications are characterized by bursty transfers of large graphics files and shared data requirements.

- Sequential editing of a single graphics image by multiple graphics artists requires file-locking middleware to ensure data integrity.

LAN-Free and Server-Free Tape Backup

- Tape backup across the messaging LAN does not provide the bandwidth to meet ever growing storage requirements.

- Implementing a SAN to accommodate backup traffic can occur in mixed parallel SCSI and Fibre Channel environments.

- Third Party Copy and NDMP solutions allow tape backups to occur without impacting server resources.

Server Clustering

- Server clustering provides both failover and load-balancing solutions for high-availability requirements.

- Servers monitor one another's status via a heartbeat protocol, typically over Ethernet.

- Fibre Channel provides shared access to storage for both load-balancing and failover implementations.

Internet Service Providers

- ISP applications require high availability to large amounts of data.

- Domain Name Systems (DNS) allow one server to assume transactions for another.

- Fibre Channel allows multiple servers to access the same storage, which is particularly important for e-commerce applications.

Campus Storage Networks

- Distributed servers and storage in a campus configuration incur administrative overhead and restrict data sharing.

- Centralizing all storage in a data center places additional burdens on the wide area network and may affect response time.

- SANs offer a compromise between distributed and centralized requirements by connecting remote servers and storage to the data center over 100MBps links.

Disaster Recovery

- Disaster recovery is facilitated by Fibre Channel's support of 10-km links.

- Fibre Channel extenders can drive distances beyond 60 km.

- High availability is augmented by provisioning both production and disaster-recovery sites with redundant SAN data paths.

- Redundant data at the disaster-recovery site can be leveraged for nondisruptive tape backup.

Fibre Channel Futures

As a standards-based architecture, Fibre Channel was originally conceived as a scalable, high-speed transport that could evolve to more enhanced functionality and performance. Cooperative efforts by researchers, vendors, and customers in the ANSI standards committees and the work of such industry organizations as the Storage Networking Industry Association (SNIA) are extending the capabilities of Fibre Channel SAN technology and storage management applications to support it. Ongoing development in upper layer protocol support, virtual circuits, multicast, security, bandwidth, and other areas will provide SAN implementers with additional options for storage network design.

9.1 Bandwidth

First implemented in quarter-speed (266Mbps) format, the majority of installations today are based on 1Gb speed, with 2Gb and 4Gb technologies under development, as well as autosensing techniques to adjust the transmission rate among 1Gb, 2Gb, and 4Gb SAN components. Doubling and quadrupling gigabit speeds poses considerable challenges for physical-layer designs, since these much higher data rates must be accomplished within Fibre Channel's 10^{-12} bit error allowance. Transceivers, connectors, cabling, and serializing/deserializing circuitry must meet much more rigid specifications to accommodate transmission rates of 2Gb and 4Gb. Loop hubs and fabric switch designs, which already require careful engineering to overcome EMI issues at 1Gb speeds, require more sophisticated approaches to meet jitter and EMI standards for higher speeds.

Proposals for autosensing techniques for automatically adjusting the transmission rate between 1Gb and variable gigabit devices will help establish compatibility between first- and second-generation products. Similar to 10/100Mbps Ethernet switches, two options are available for accommodating lower data rates. Some Ethernet switch products simply drop the transmission rate of the entire switch to 10Mbps when a slower device is attached. This eliminates any buffering issues when, for example, a 100Mbps device sends packets to a 10Mbps device. Higher-end 10/100Mbps switches allow attachment of both 10Mbps and 100Mbps products and provide sufficient buffering within the switch to queue up packets for the slower links. The same principle applies to multispeed Fibre Channel switches, since accommodating both 1Gbps and 2Gbps or 4Gbps nodes on a single switch will require significant buffering to avoid frame loss. As depicted in Figure 9-1, a likely implementation for multiple-speed Fibre

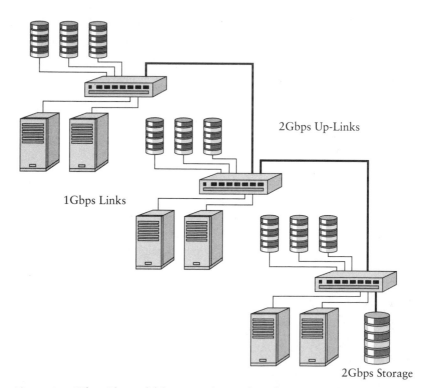

Figure 9-1 *Fibre Channel fabric switches with 1Gbps and 2Gbps support*

Channel fabrics is the use of higher-speed links to eliminate bottlenecks in switch-to-switch configurations.

9.2 Fibre Channel over Wide Area Networking

For the SAN interconnect, the adoption of Fibre Channel technology in enterprise networks naturally leads to the issue of connectivity between isolated SANs across a wide area network. Fibre Channel–to–ATM router modules will allow islands of storage networks to be integrated into an enterprisewide SAN, thus offering additional options for data sharing, disaster recovery, and backup operations. The impetus for these products is fed by the major LAN and WAN vendors, which are reaching toward the SAN from an established base of backbone routers, and the Fibre Channel fabric switch vendors, which see router technology as a means to extend SANs over regional distances. As shown in Figure 9-2, fabric switches with Fibre Channel–to–ATM modules allow an enterprise to share data between remote locations by tunneling Fibre Channel protocol within a switched ATM transport.

9.3 Coexistence within Enterprise Networks

The evolution of Fibre Channel technology is following the model previously established by Ethernet and Token Ring LANs, in which the

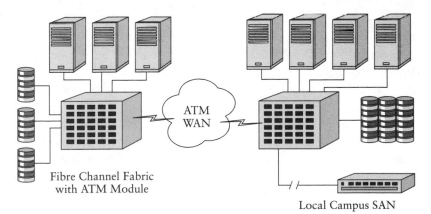

Figure 9-2 *Fibre Channel across an ATM wide area network*

introduction of higher speeds occurred within an installed base of relatively slower-speed infrastructures. Since no customer wants to or can afford simply to scrap the previous-generation products, the adoption of a higher-speed or more fully featured technology is driven more by specific application requirements than by new-product availability. For example, 100Mbps switched Ethernet was originally deployed primarily for up-links between 10Mbps hubs or switches, thus eliminating congestion between floors or between clusters of users and common servers. As 100Mbps switches and 10/100Mbps adapters became more affordable, 100Mbps Ethernet gradually displaced 10Mbps Ethernet for desktop applications. Where did the 10Mbps hubs and switches go? In large enterprises, they migrated to less mission-critical or bandwidth-intensive areas. Now, the former state-of-the-art 100Mbps switches are being pushed down through the enterprise by the introduction of Gigabit Ethernet at the top. This migration preserves the customer's investment in technology while the process of displacement gradually upgrades the entire network. The most remarkable aspect of this process today is the speed with which the displacement is occurring.

Every new infrastructure that displaces an incumbent refers to the previous occupant as a "legacy," or dead-end, technology. Mainframe data processing, for example, was declared a legacy system by the advocates of PC-based client/server applications and hardware. SNA is legacy in terms of TCP/IP, although both have substantial histories. Shared 10Mbps Ethernet hubs are legacy products compared to 100Mbps Ethernet switches. After 20 years of existence, parallel SCSI-based disk drives and HBAs are commonly referred to as legacy products, primarily by the advocates of Fibre Channel and other high-speed transports. And although Fibre Channel products have been installed in production environments for only a few years, Fibre Channel itself has acquired a legacy base. Quarter-speed transceivers and switches are legacy products. Fibre Channel Arbitrated Loop disk drives and HBAs that do not support fabric services are legacy products, now that viable fabric switches are shipping. Unmanaged loop hubs will soon become legacy products, as the adoption of SANs for enterprise applications raises consciousness of management and loop integrity issues. Like driving a brand new car off the sales lot, every new technology seemingly depreciates as soon as it falls into the hands of the willing consumer.

Nonetheless, mainframes are thriving; SNA is still used in mission-critical environments, even though it may be wrapped in IP as a transport protocol; client/server applications and hardware are invading every aspect of commerce; the markets for 10Mbps Ethernet hubs, 100Mbps switches, and Gigabit Ethernet are all thriving; sales of parallel SCSI continue to climb; and quarter-speed and nonfabric Fibre Channel products continue to lead productive lives even while new managed hub and fabric switch products ship in the tens of thousands. The bottom line to all these realities is that the IT market is simply too massive and too varied to be overthrown by the introduction of any single technological solution.

Application requirements drive the introduction of new hardware and software. For the wide variety of storage applications in large and small enterprises, a number of architectures will continue to satisfy user needs. Parallel SCSI, SCSI switches, higher-performance LVD (low-voltage differential) SCSI, FireWire, new next-generation or future I/O products, Fibre Channel hubs, fabric switches, and arrays will all find homes in mainstream or niche storage environments, depending on bandwidth, distance, device population, scalability, cost, and other qualifying issues.

9.4 Interoperability

The viability of Fibre Channel SANs has been affirmed by customers and solutions providers that have installed SAN configurations to resolve tape backup, high-bandwidth, server-clustering, high-capacity storage, and distance issues. Solution providers necessarily assume responsibility for qualifying interoperability for the product suites they deploy, whereas the self-interest of point-product (HBA, disk, hub, or switch) vendors promotes interoperability to ensure the success of their own products. The first major threshold for multivendor interoperability was crossed with Arbitrated Loop–based products. The second is being addressed by interoperability between fabric switches for multivendor enterprise SANs. The next threshold will be defined by multispeed products that combine 1Gb, 2Gb, and 4Gb links with autosensing algorithms to connect 1Gb devices with 2Gb- and 4Gb-capable switches and hubs. In addition to sheer bandwidth, further definition of, for example, extended services, class of service, support for IP, and Virtual Interface protocols, exerts pressure on all parties to both abide by standards and validate interoperable implementations. As in local and wide area networking, interoperability is accelerated by customer need and the purchasing power that enforces compliance.

9.5 Total SAN Solutions

Deploying a high-speed interconnect alone may quickly resolve specific bandwidth issues but does not leverage the greater potential of a SAN. That potential is realized by the integration of new storage management, storage resource management, interconnect management, server clustering, and other superstructure applications that are facilitated by the underlying SAN architecture. Large enterprise networks can normally justify installation of new management applications and infrastructure if they reduce overall administrative costs, simplify day-to-day operations, and contribute to high-availability and proactive capacity planning. Cooperation and partnerships among storage management software vendors, application vendors, and vendors of Fibre Channel hardware are engendering comprehensive solutions that can fulfill both transport and management needs.

9.6 Summary

Bandwidth

- Higher-speed 2Gb and 4Gb Fibre Channel transports will convenience high-performance interswitch links.

- Combining a 1Gb device with 2Gb- or 4Gb-capable switches will require autosensing logic and potentially greater buffering.

Fibre Channel over Wide Area Networking

- Fibre Channel–to–ATM or other wide area links will allow SANs to be extended over far greater distances for enterprisewide implementations.

- Both router vendors and SAN interconnect vendors are driving the SAN-to-WAN initiative.

Coexistence within Enterprise Networks

- The introduction of Fibre Channel–based SAN technology will gradually displace some traditional SCSI infrastructures at the middle and high end of the market but will coexist with legacy technologies for some time to come.

Interoperability

- Interoperability is being driven by customer demand.

- SAN interconnect and software vendors have a vested interest in ensuring that their products are standards-based and interoperable.

Total SAN Solutions

- The power of storage area networks is realized by the integration of interconnect hardware and storage management software.

Appendix A
Fibre Channel Ordered Sets

Set	Code
Primitive Signals	
Arbitrate	ARB(x)
Fairness/Initialization	ARB(F0)
IDLE alternative	ARB(FF)
Close	CLS
Dynamic Half Duplex	DHD
Idle	IDLE
Mark	MRK(tx)
Open Full Duplex	OPN(yx)
Open Half Duplex	OPN(yy)
Open Selective Replicate	OPN(yr)
Receiver Ready	R_RDY
Primitive Sequences	
Link Reset	LR
Link Reset Response	LRR
Loop Initialization	LIP
Loop Failure, no AL_PA	LIP(F8,F7)
Loop Failure, valid AL_PA	LIP(F8, AL_PS)
Initialization, no AL_PA	LIP(F7,F7)
Initialization, valid AL_PA	LIP(F7, AL_PS)
Selective Reset	LIP(AL_PD, AL_PS)

(*continued*)

Set	Code
Primitive Sequences (*continued*)	
Loop Port Bypass	LPB
Loop Port Bypass—selected port	LPB(yx)
Loop Port Bypass—all ports	LPB(fx)
Loop Port Enable	LPE.
Loop Port Enable—selected port	LPE(yx)
Loop Port Enable—all ports	LPE(fx)
Not Operational	NOS
Off-line State	OLS
Frame Delimiters	
Start of Frame—Connect Class 1	SOFc1
Start of Frame—Initiate Class 1	SOFi1
Start of Frame—Normal Class 1	SOFn1
Start of Frame—Initiate Class 2	SOFi2
Start of Frame—Normal Class 2	SOFn2
Start of Frame—Initiate Class 3	SOFi3
Start of Frame—Normal Class 3	SOFn3
Start of Frame—Activate Class 4	SOFc4
Start of Frame—Initiate Class 4	SOFi4
Start of Frame—Normal Class 4	SOFn4
Start of Frame—Initiate Loop	SOFiL
End of Frame—Normal	EOFn
End of Frame—Terminate	EOFt
End of Frame—Disconnect Terminate Class 1	EOFdt
End of Frame—Deactivate Terminate Class 4	EOFdt
End of Frame—Abort	EOFa
End of Frame—Normal Invalid	EOFni

(*continued*)

Set	Code
Frame Delimiters (*continued*)	
End of Frame—Disconnect Terminal Invalid Class 1	EOFdti
End of Frame—Deactivate Terminate Invalid Class 4	EOFdti
End of Frame—Remove Terminate Class 4	EOFrt
End of Frame—Remove Terminate Invalid Class 4	EOFrti

Appendix B
Fibre Channel Vendors

Product	Web Site URL
Transceivers	
AMP	www.amp.com
Finisar Corporation	www.finisar.com
Fujikura	www.fujikura.com
Hewlett Packard	www.hp.com
Methode Electronics	www.methode.com
Vixel Corporation	www.vixel.com
Media Interface Adapters	
Methode Electronics	www.methode.com
W. L. Gore & Associates	www.gore.com
Host Bus Adapters	
Atto Technology	www.attotech.com
Emulex Corporation	www.emulex.com
GENROCO	www.genroco.com
Hewlett Packard	www.hp.com
Interphase Corporation	www.iphase.com
Jaycor Networks	www.jni.com
LSILogic (Symbios)	www.lsilogic.com
Prisa Networks	www.prisa.com
QLogic Corporation	www.qlc.com
Troika Networks	www.troikanetworks.com

(*continued*)

Product	Web Site URL
Loop Hubs	
Atto Technology	www.attotech.com
Emulex Corporation	www.emulex.com
G2 Networks	www.g2networks.com
Gadzoox Networks	www.gadzoox.com
Vixel Corporation	www.vixel.com
Fabric Switches	
Ancor Communications	www.ancor.com
Brocade Communications Systems	www.brocade.com
McData Corporation	www.mcdata.com
Vixel Corporation	www.vixel.com
Fibre Channel–SCSI Bridges	
Atto Technology	www.attotech.com
Chaparral Technologies	www.chaparraltec.com
Crossroads Systems	www.crossroads.com
RAID/JBOD/Tape Subsystems	
ADIC	www.adic.com
Andataco	www.andataco.com
Artecon	www.artecon.com
ATL Products	www.atlp.com
BoxHill Systems Corporation	www.boxhill.com
Ciprico	www.ciprico.com
Data General CLARiiON	www.clariion.com
DataDirect Networks	www.datadirectnetworks.com
Distributed Processing Technology	www.dpt.com
ECCS	www.eccs.com
EMC Corporation	www.emc.com

(*continued*)

Product	Web Site URL
RAID/JBOD/Tape Subsystems (*continued*)	
Eurologic	www.eurologic.com
Exabyte Corporation	www.exabyte.com
Hitachi Data Systems	www.hds.com
Infortrend Technologies	www.iftraid.com
JMR Electronics	www.jmr.com
Maxstrat	www.maxstrat.com
MountainGate Imaging Systems	www.mountaingate.com
MTI Technology Corporation	www.mti.com
Mylex	www.mylex.com
Nstor	www.nstor.com
OneofUs Company	www.oneofus.com
Overland Data	www.overlanddata.com
Procom Technology	www.procom.com
Raidtec Corporation	www.raidtec.com
Seagate Technology	www.seagate.com
StorageTek	www.network.com

Fibre Channel Systems	
Amdahl Corporation	www.amdahl.com
Avid Sports	www.avidsports.com
Avid Technology	www.avid.com
Bull Information Systems	www.bull.com
Compaq Computer Corporation	www.compaq.com
Dell Computer Corporation	www.dell.com
IBM Corporation	www.ibm.com
Intergraph Corporation	www.ingr.com
NCR	www.ncr.com

(*continued*)

Product	Web Site URL
Fibre Channel Systems (*continued*)	
Sequent Computer Systems	www.sequent.com
Siemens Nixdorf	www.sni.com
Silicon Graphics	www.sgi.com
Sun Microsystems	www.sun.com
Tektronix	www.tek.com
Unisys Corporation	www.unisys.com
Management Software	
CrosStor	www.crosstor.com
HighGround Systems	www.highground.com
Intelliguard Software	www.iguard.com
Legato Systems	www.legato.com
Mercury Computer Systems	www.mc.com
Transoft Technology Corporation	www.transoft.com
Veritas Software	www.veritas.com
Analyzers/Test/Independent Labs	
Ancot Corporation	www.ancot.com
Finisar Corporation	www.finisar.com
I-Tech Corporation	www.i-tech.com
Medusa Labs	www.medusalabs.com
University of New Hampshire	www.unh.edu
Xyratex Test Systems	www.xyratex.com

Bibliography

References

Benner, Alan F. *Fibre Channel*. McGraw-Hill, New York, 1996.

Kembel, Robert W. *The Fibre Channel Consultant: Arbitrated Loop*, Northwest Learning Associates, Tucson, AZ, 1997.

————. *The Fibre Channel Consultant: A Comprehensive Introduction*, Northwest Learning Associates, Tucson, AZ, 1998.

Stai, Jeffrey D. *The Fibre Channel Bench Reference*, ENDL Publications, Saratoga, CA, 1996.

Standards and Proposals

Available in hardcopy from Global Engineering, 15 Inverness Way East, Englewood, CO 80112.

FC-AL, *Fibre Channel Arbitrated Loop*, ANSI X3.272-1996.

FC-AL-2, *Fibre Channel Arbitrated Loop*, ANSI X3.T11 Project 1133-D.

FC-GS, *Fibre Channel Generic Services*, ANSI X3.288-1996.

FC-GS-2, *Fibre Channel Generic Services 2*, ANSI X3.T11 Project 1134-D.

FC-LE, *Fibre Channel Link Encapsulation*, ANSI X3.287-1996.

FC-PH, *Fibre Channel Physical and Signaling Interface*, ANSI X3.230-1994.

FC-PH Errata, *Fibre Channel Physical and Signaling Interface Errata*, ANSI X3.230:AM1-1996.

FC-PH-2, *Fibre Channel Physical and Signaling Interface-2*, ANSI X3.297-1997.

FC-PH-3, *Fibre Channel Physical and Signaling Interface-3,* ANSI X3.T11 Project 1119-D.

FC-SL, *Fibre Channel Slotted Loop,* ANSI X3.T11 Project 1232-D.

FC-SW, *Fibre Channel Switch Fabric,* ANSI X3.T11 Project 959-D.

FCP, *Fibre Channel Protocol for SCSI,* ANSI X3.269-199*x*.

Web Resources

www.fibrechannel.com (Fibre Channel Association)

www.fcloop.org (Fibre Channel Loop Community)

www.T11.org (ANSI T11 Organization)

www.iol.unh.edu/consortiums/fc (University of New Hampshire)

www.cern.ch/HSI/fcs (European Laboratory for Particle Physics)

www.snia.org (Storage Networking Industry Association)

Glossary

Access fairness A process by which contending nodes are guaranteed access to an Arbitrated Loop.

Access method The means used to access a physical medium in order to transmit data.

Active copper A Fibre Channel connection that allows up to 30-m copper cabling between devices.

Address identifier A 24-bit value used to indicate the link-level address of communicating devices. In a frame header, the address identifier indicates the source ID (S_ID) and destination ID (D_ID) of the frame.

AL_PA Arbitrated Loop Physical Address; an 8-bit value used to identify a participating device in an Arbitrated Loop.

ANSI American National Standards Institute; governing body for standards in the United States.

Arbitrated Loop A shared 100MBps Fibre Channel transport supporting up to 126 devices and 1 fabric attachment.

Arbitration A means for gaining orderly access to a shared-loop topology.

ARP Address Resolution Protocol; an IP function that correlates an IP network address to a link-level MAC address.

ASIC Application-specific integrated circuit.

ATM Asynchronous transfer mode; a high-speed cell-switching transport used primarily in wide area networks.

Bandwidth Transmission capacity of a link or a system.

BB_Credit Buffer-to-buffer credit; used to determine how many frames can be sent to a recipient.

Bypass circuitry Circuits that automatically remove a device from the data path when valid signaling is lost.

Cascade Connecting two or more Fibre Channel hubs or fabric switches to increase the number of ports or to extend distances.

CDR Clock and data recovery circuitry.

CIM Common Information Model; a management structure enabling disparate resources to be managed by a common application.

Class 1 A connection-oriented class of service that requires acknowledgment of frame delivery.

Class 2 A connectionless class of service that requires acknowledgment of frame delivery.

Class 3 A connectionless class of service that requires no notification of frame delivery.

Class 4 A class of service that defines virtual circuits via fractional bandwidth and quality-of-service parameters.

Class 6 A class of service that provides multicast frame delivery with acknowledgment.

CRC Cyclic redundancy check; an error-detection method.

Cut-through A switching technique that allows a routing decision to be made as soon as the destination address of a frame is received.

Disparity The relationship of 1s and 0s in an encoded character: positive disparity contains more 1s; negative disparity contains more 0s; neutral disparity contains an even number of 1s and 0s.

EE_Credit End-to-end credit; used to manage the exchange of frames by two communicating devices.

E_Port An expansion port connecting two fabric switches.

8b/10b encoding An encoding scheme that converts an 8-bit byte into two possible 10-bit characters; used for balancing 1s and 0s in high-speed transports.

EOF End of frame; a group of ordered sets used to delineate the end of a frame.

F_Port On a Fibre Channel switch, a port that supports an N_Port.

FL_Port On a Fibre Channel switch, a port that supports Arbitrated Loop devices.

FLOGI Fabric Login; a process by which a node establishes a logical connection to a fabric switch.

Fabric One or more Fibre Channel switches in a networked topology.

Frame A data unit comprising a start-of-frame delimiter, header, data payload, CRC, and end-of-frame delimiter.

Full duplex Concurrent transmission and reception of data on a link.

G_Port On a Fibre Channel switch, a port that supports either F_Port or E_Port functionality.

GBIC Gigabit interface converter; a removable transceiver module for Fibre Channel and Gigabit Ethernet physical-layer transport.

Gbps Gigabits per second.

Gigabit For Fibre Channel, 1,062,500,000 bits per second.

GLM Gigabit link module; a semipermanent transceiver that incorporates serializing/deserializing functions.

HBA Host bus adapter; an interface between a server or workstation bus and the Fibre Channel network.

HiPPI High-performance parallel interface; a high-speed interface normally used in supercomputer environments.

HSSDC High-speed serial direct connect; a form factor that allows quick connect/disconnect for copper interfaces.

HTTP HyperText Transfer Protocol.

Hub In Fibre Channel, a wiring concentrator that collapses a loop topology into a physical star topology.

IP Internet Protocol.

In-band Transmission of management protocol over the Fibre Channel transport.

Initiator On a Fibre Channel network, typically a server or a workstation that initiates transactions to disk or tape targets.

Intercabinet A specification for copper cabling that allows up to 30-m distance between enclosures.

Intermix Allows any unused bandwidth in a Class 1 connection to be used by Class 2 or Class 3 transactions.

Intracabinet A specification for copper cabling that allows up to 13-m distance within a single enclosure.

ISP Internet service provider.

JBOD Just a bunch of disks; typically configured as an Arbitrated Loop segment in a single chassis.

Jitter Deviation in timing that a bit stream encounters as it traverses a physical medium.

K28.5 A special 10-bit character used to indicate the beginning of a Fibre Channel command.

LAN Local area network; a network linking multiple devices in a single geographical location.

LED Light-emitting diode; a status indicator on an interconnect device.

LIP Loop Initialization Primitive; used to initiate a procedure that results in unique addressing for all nodes, to indicate a loop failure, or to reset a specific node.

LISM Loop Initialization Select Master; a process by which a temporary loop master is determined.

Loop Port State Machine Logic that monitors and performs the tasks required for initialization and access to the loop.

Mbps Megabits per second.

MBps Megabytes per second.

MIA Media interface adapter; a device that converts optical signaling to electrical.

MIB Management Information Base; an SNMP structure for device management.

MTBF Mean time between failure.

Multimode A fiber-optic cabling specification that allows up to 500-m distance between devices.

N_Port A Fibre Channel port in a point-to-point or fabric connection.

NAS Network-attached storage; a disk array connected to a controller that provides connection to a LAN transport.

NDMP Network Data Management Protocol; a protocol for performing tape backups without consuming server resources.

NL_Port Node loop port; a port that supports Arbitrated Loop protocol.

Node A Fibre Channel entity that supports one or more ports.

Node_Name A unique 64-bit identifier assigned to a Fibre Channel Node.

Non-OFC Laser transceivers whose lower-intensity output does not require special OFC mechanisms.

OFC Open fiber control; a method used to disable and enable laser signaling for higher-intensity laser transceivers.

OLTP Online transaction processing.

Ordered Set A group of low-level protocols used to manage frame transport, initialization, and media access.

Out-of-band Transmission of management protocol outside of the Fibre Channel network, typically over Ethernet.

Parallel The simultaneous transmission of multiple data bits over multiple lines.

Passive copper A low-cost Fibre Channel connection that allows up to 13-m copper cable lengths.

PLOGI A port-to-port login process by which initiators establish sessions with targets.

Point to point A dedicated Fibre Channel connection between two devices.

Port A Fibre Channel physical entity that connects a node to the network.

Port_Name A unique 64-bit identifier assigned to a Fibre Channel port.

Primitive Sequences Ordered sets that indicate or initiate state changes on the transport and require at least three consecutive occurrences to trigger a response.

Primitive signals Ordered sets that indicate actions or events and require only one occurrence to trigger response.

Private loop A free-standing Arbitrated Loop with no fabric attachment.

Private loop device An Arbitrated Loop device that does not support fabric login.

Public loop An Arbitrated Loop attached to a fabric switch.

Public loop device An Arbitrated Loop device that supports fabric login and services.

RAID Redundant Array of Independent Disks.

Repeater A circuit that uses recovered clock to regenerate the outbound signal.

Retimer A circuit that uses an independent clock to generate an outbound signal.

RSCN Registered State Change Notification; a switch function that allows notification to registered nodes if a change occurs to other, specified nodes.

SAN Storage area network; a network linking servers or workstations to disk arrays, tape-backup subsystems, and other devices, typically over Fibre Channel.

SCSI Small Computer Systems Interface; both a protocol for transmitting large blocks of data and a parallel bus architecture.

SCSI-3 A SCSI standard that defines transmission of SCSI protocol over serial links.

SERDES Serialing/deserializing circuitry; a circuit that converts a serial bit stream into parallel data characters, and parallel into serial.

Serial The transmission of data bits in sequential order over a single line.

Server A computer that processes end-user requests for data and/or applications.

SES SCSI Enclosure Services; a subset of SCSI protocol used to monitor power, temperature, and fan status of enclosures.

Single mode A fiber-optic cabling specification that provides up to 10-km distance between devices.

SMI Structure of Management Information; a notation for setting or retrieving management variables over SNMP.

SNMP Simple Network Management Protocol; a network management protocol designed to run over TCP/IP routed networks.

SNS Simple Name Server; provided by a fabric switch, a service that simplifies discovery of devices.

SOF Start of Frame; a group of ordered sets that delineate the beginning of a frame.

SRM Storage resource management; management of disk volumes and file resources.

Storage Any device used to store data; typically, magnetic disk media or tape.

Store-and-forward A switching technique that requires buffering an entire frame before a routing decision is made.

Striping A RAID technique for writing a single file to multiple disks on a block-by-block basis.

Switch A device providing full bandwidth per port and high-speed routing of data via link-level addressing.

Target Typically a disk array or a tape subsystem on a Fibre Channel network.

TCP/IP Transmission Control Protocol over Internet Protocol.

TELNET A virtual terminal emulation facility over TCP/IP.

Tenancy Possession of an Arbitrated Loop by a device to conduct a transaction.

Topology The physical or logical arrangement of devices in a networked configuration.

TPC Third Party Copy; a protocol for performing tape backups without consuming server resources.

Transceiver A device that converts one form of signaling to another for both transmission and reception; in fiber optics, conversion from optical to electrical.

VAR Value-added reseller.

WAN Wide area network; a network linking geographically remote sites.

World-Wide Name A registered, unique 64-bit identifier assigned to nodes and ports.

Zoning Provided by fabric switches or hubs, a function that allows segregation of node by physical port, name, or address.

Index